Tennessee

A STREETCAR NAMED DESIRE

Edited by Ray Speakman

THE HEREFORD PLAYS

HEINEMANN · METHUEN

HEREFORD PLAYS

Heinemann Educational Books Ltd
Halley Court, Jordan Hill, Oxford OX2 8EJ
OXFORD LONDON EDINBURGH
MELBOURNE SYDNEY AUCKLAND
IBADAN NAIROBI GABORONE HARARE
KINGSTON PORTSMOUTH NH (USA)
SINGAPORE MADRID

First published by Methuen in 1984 by arrangement with
Secker and Warburg Ltd.

First published in this edition by Heinemann/Methuen 1989

93 94 95 96 97 11 10 9 8 7 6 5 4 3 2

Copyright © 1947 by the Estate of the late Tennessee Williams
Introduction and notes copyright © Ray Speakman 1989

Typeset by
Taurus Graphics, Abingdon, Oxfordshire
Printed in England by Clays Ltd, St Ives plc

Contents

INTRODUCTION

Tennessee Williams and A Streetcar Named Desire

Thomas Lanier Williams was born in Columbus, Mississippi on March 26th, 1911. He assumed the name 'Tennessee' in 1938 because, he said, "The Williams's fought the Indians for Tennessee, and I had already discovered that the life of a young writer was going to be something similar to the defence of the stockade against a band of savages" – a description reminiscent of Blanche's battles with Stanley in *A Streetcar Named Desire*. Indeed, it has been repeatedly pointed out by critics, biographers and Williams himself, that his plays were very much an exploration and a working out of his own life.

His father, Cornelius Coffin Williams, a hard drinking, bad tempered, coarse man who called his son "Miss Nancy", was often absent from the household – he had "fallen in love with long distances" like the father in *The Glass Menagerie* – in his work for the telephone company, and later, for a shoe company. Tennessee's mother was Edwina Dakin, the daughter of an Episcopal minister. She despised her husband's drinking and womanising; she felt she had an aristocratic pedigree which was ill suited to the life her husband, and his frequent changes of address, forced her to lead. 'CC' Williams and Edwina Dakin had three children: Rose, born in 1907, Tom, born in 1911 and Dakin, born in 1919 – shortly after the family's traumatic move to St Louis. In St Louis the family were separated from Edwina's genteel background – she was thirty-four and had to cook for the first time – an experience which Tom later described as losing "belief in everything but loss". As a result, Tom withdrew into his writing, Edwina into dreams of lost Southern gentility, and Tom's sister,

Rose, into madness – she was lobotomized in 1937. Edwina Dakin Williams, similarly, ended her life in a mental home.

Tennessee Williams's first major success was *The Glass Menagerie* (1944), his second was *A Streetcar Named Desire* (1947). In an article in the *New York Times* (30 11 47) Williams describes the disadvantages of sudden fame, – "the catastrophe of success," which he had experienced following his first successful play. He felt that the material security he found following *The Glass Menagerie* had limited his creativity. He felt that *Streetcar* rediscovered this creativity – and in many ways this battle between humanity and the corrupting effect of security is an important theme in the play.

When *Streetcar* was first performed in England in 1949 it attracted a good deal of the 'wrong' sort of attention: it was serialised in one of the more excitable Sunday newspapers and was popularly thought to be sexually permissive in the extreme. The play's early reputation, however, was short lived; critics and audiences alike quickly came to see Williams's play for what it really is – a work of great humanity and technical brilliance. Indeed, it is not too grand a claim to suggest that *A Streetcar Named Desire* is a classic tragedy. The poet Keats identified a tragic hero as an individual unable to see that life has its impossibilities. Tennessee Williams's contemporary, Arthur Miller, maintained that the struggle of a tragic hero, "is that of the individual attempting to gain his rightful place in society . . . ready to lay down his life, if need be, to secure one thing – his sense of personal dignity." Keats and Miller would, I think, have recognised in Blanche the individual they had in mind – unable to renounce the image of herself as a rare being, unable to accept, as her sister does, the "blisses of the commonplace".

Between his success with *Streetcar* and 1962 Tennessee Williams produced a large number of highly acclaimed plays: *Summer and Smoke* (1948), *The Rose Tattoo* (1951), *Camino Real* (1953), *Cat on a Hot Tin Roof* (1955), *Orpheus Descending* (1957), *Suddenly Last Summer* (1958), *Sweet Bird of Youth* (1959), *Period of Adjustment* (1960), *Night of the Iguana* (1961) and *The Milk Train Doesn't Stop Here Anymore* (1962). *Night of the Iguana* is considered by many to be his last great play, and although his reputation declined in subsequent years, he continued writing until his death (by accidentally choking on a bottle top) in 1983.

In 1976 Williams published his *Memoirs*. He wrote to his agent shortly before their publication: "I have a new title for my memoirs – 'Flee, Flee This Sad Hotel' – it's a quote from a poem by Anne Sexton. Of course hotel is a metaphor for my life – and flight from it – if not an impulse – at least is an imminence." He never used the title.

Following the text of the play you will find a series of **Activities and Explorations**. Although these are by no means exhaustive, they are, inevitably, fairly detailed. Their purpose is to encourage a close reading of the text and to stimulate thought, discussion and writing. Many of the suggestions for assignments are shaped with GCSE coursework and A level critical essays in mind.

Whatever your purpose in reading the play, you will find *A Streetcar Named Desire* eminently approachable, and a richly rewarding play to study in depth.

Ray Speakman

Further Reading and References

File on Tennessee Williams (Methuen, 1988)

Monsters in the Menagerie John Lahr, (*The Guardian*, 2.2.88)

Talk About America 1951–1968 Alistair Cooke (Penguin, 1981)

The Language of Modern Drama Gareth Lloyd Evans (Dent, 1977)

Latecomers Anita Brookner (Jonathan Cape, 1988)

A Streetcar Named Desire, with commentary and notes Patricia Hearn (Methuen, 1984)

A Streetcar Named Desire: a Study in Ambiguity An essay by John Gassner in *Modern Drama* (OUP, 1965)

Remember Me to Tom Edwina Dakin Williams and Lucy Freeman (Putnam's, New York, 1963)

Tennessee Williams: A Tribute edited by J. Tharpe (University Press of Mississippi, 1977)

Twentieth Century Interpretations of *Streetcar* edited by J. Y. Miller (Prentice-Hall, 1971)

Works which might be looked at alongside *A Streetcar Named Desire*:

The Glass Menagerie Tennessee Williams (Heinemann Educational 1970)

All My Sons Arthur Miller (Heinemann Educational 1971)

Miss Julie August Strindberg (1888)

The Cherry Orchard Anton Chekhov (1903)

The Widowing of Mrs Holroyd and The Daughter-in-Law D. H. Lawrence (Heinemann Educational 1988

Sons and Lovers D. H. Lawrence

CHARACTERS

① The whole of Blanche's life is given over to play acting, not only out of necessity but for its own sake. Rare moments when she speaks the plain, unvarnished truth are Jarring and shocking.

② We are aware of the fear beneath the brittle chatter. There is always a threat of hysteria, whether she is telling a funny story or remembering the terrible last days at Belle Reve and this is what gives the play its dramatic tension.

③ Blanche makes no blatant bids for our sympathy. She's snobbish + critical + selfish. Even more sympathetic towards Stanley.

STANLEY

① No life outside the play like Blanche.

② Though uneducated, he is no fool.

③ Leads his friends

④ Opposite to Blanche in every way

STELLA

Grows into an intriguing character. Not certain about her background. Only thing we do know is that she is passionately attached to Stanley.

Strong sexuality is characteristic in both sisters but Stella is open about her feelings

Stella is presented with a choice - Belle Reve vs New Orleans, Blanche vs Stanley

She seals Blanche's fate.

blue Piano - New Orleans . Polka - old world

A STREETCAR NAMED DESIRE

And so it was I entered the broken world
To trace the visionary company of love, its voice
An instant in the wind (I know not whither hurled)
But not for long to hold each desperate choice.
               "THE BROKEN TOWER" BY HART CRANE

THE CHARACTERS

BLANCHE
STELLA
STANLEY
MITCH
EUNICE
STEVE
PABLO
A NEGRO WOMAN
A DOCTOR
A NURSE
A YOUNG COLLECTOR
A MEXICAN WOMAN
A TAMALE VENDOR

The first London production of this play was at the Aldwych Theatre on Wednesday, October 12th, 1949, with the following cast:

BLANCHE DUBOIS	Vivien Leigh
STELLA KOWALSKI	Renee Asherson
STANLEY KOWALSKI	Bonar Colleano
HAROLD MITCHELL (MITCH)	Bernard Braden
EUNICE HUBBEL	Eileen Dale
STEVE HUBBEL	Lyn Evans
PABLO GONZALES	Theodore Bikel
NEGRO WOMAN	Bruce Howard
A STRANGE MAN (DOCTOR)	Sidney Monckton
A STRANGE WOMAN (NURSE)	Mona Lilian
A YOUNG COLLECTOR	John Forrest
A MEXICAN WOMAN	Eileen Way

Directed by LAURENCE OLIVER
Setting and lighting by JO MIELZINER
Costumes by BEATRICE DAWSON

SCENE I

The exterior of a two-storey corner building on a street in New Orleans which is named Elysian Fields and runs between the L & N tracks and the river. The section is poor but, unlike corresponding sections in other American cities, it has a raffish charm. The houses are mostly white frame, weathered grey, with rickety outside stairs and galleries and quaintly ornamented gables to the entrances of both. It is first dark of an evening early in May. The sky that shows around the dim white building is a peculiarly tender blue, almost turquoise, which invests the scene with a kind of lyricism and gracefully attenuates the atmosphere of decay. You can almost feel the warm breath of the brown river beyond the river warehouses with their faint redolences of bananas and coffee. A corresponding air is evoked by the music of Negro entertainers at a bar-room around the corner. In this part of New Orleans you are practically always just around the corner, or a few doors down the street, from a tinny piano being played with the infatuated fluency of brown fingers. This "Blue Piano" expresses the spirit of the life which goes on here.

Two women, one white and one coloured, are taking the air on the steps of the building. The white woman is EUNICE, *who occupies the upstairs flat; the coloured woman a neighbour, for New Orleans is a cosmopolitan city where there is a relatively warm and easy intermingling of races in the old part of town. Above the music of the "Blue Piano" the voices of people on the street can be heard overlapping.*

1

NEGRO WOMAN (*to* EUNICE): . . . she says St. Barnabas would send out his dog to lick her and when he did she'd feel an icy cold wave all up an' down her. Well, that night when –

A MAN (*to a* SAILOR): You keep right on going and you'll find it. You'll hear them tapping on the shutters.

SAILOR (*to* NEGRO WOMAN *and* EUNICE): Where's the Four Deuces?

VENDOR: Red hot! Red hots!

NEGRO WOMAN: Don't waste your money in that clip joint!

SAILOR: I've got a date there.

VENDOR: Re-e-ed h-o-o-t!

NEGRO WOMAN: Don't let them sell you a Blue Moon cocktail or you won't go out on your own feet!

Two men come around the corner, STANLEY KOWALSKI *and* MITCH. *They are about twenty-eight or thirty years old, roughly dressed in blue denim work clothes.* STANLEY *carries his bowling jacket and a red-stained package from a butchers's.*) Si full blooded

STANLEY (*to* MITCH): Well, what did he say?

MITCH: He said he'd give us even money.

STANLEY: Naw! We gotta have odds!

They stop at the foot of the steps.

STANLEY (*bellowing*): Hey, there! Stella, Baby!

STELLA *comes out on the first-floor landing, a gentle young woman, about twenty-five, and of a background obviously quite different from her husbands's.*

STELLA (*mildly*): Don't holler at me like that. Hi, Mitch.

STANLEY: Catch!

STELLA: What?

STANLEY: Meat!

He heaves the package at her. She cries out in protest but manages to catch it; then she laughs breathlessly. Her husband and his companion have already started back around the corner.

STELLA (*calling after him*): Stanley! Where are you going?
STANLEY: Bowling!
STELLA: Can I come watch?
STANLEY: Come on. (*He goes out.*)
STELLA: Be over soon. (*To the white woman.*) Hello, Eunice. How are you?
EUNICE: I'm all right. Tell Steve to get him a poor boy's sandwich 'cause nothing's left here.

They all laugh; the COLOURED WOMAN *does not stop.* STELLA *goes out.*

NEGRO WOMAN: What was that package he th'ew at 'er? (*She rises from steps, laughing louder.*)
EUNICE: You hush, now!
NEGRO WOMAN: Catch *what*!

She continues to laugh. BLANCHE *comes around the corner, carrying a valise. She looks at a slip of paper, then at the building, then again at the slip and again at the building. Her expression is one of shocked disbelief. Her appearance is incongruous to this setting. She is daintily dressed in a white suit with a fluffy bodice, necklace and earrings of pearl, white gloves and hat, looking as if she were arriving at a summer tea or cocktail party in the garden district. She is above five years older than* STELLA. *Her delicate beauty must avoid a strong light. There is something about her uncertain manner, as well as her*

3

white clothes, that suggests a moth.

EUNICE (*finally*): What's the matter, honey? Are you lost?

BLANCHE (*with faintly hysterical humour*): They told me to take a street-car named Desire, and then transfer to one called Cemeteries and ride six blocks and get off at – Elysian Fields! *Symbolic of B's life   see P.17*

[handwritten margin note: dea h / heaven]

EUNICE: That's where you are now.

BLANCHE: At Elysian Fields?

EUNICE: This here is Elysian Fields.

BLANCHE: They mustn't have – understood – what number I wanted . . .

EUNICE: What number you lookin' for?

BLANCHE *wearily refers to the slip of paper*.

BLANCHE: Six thirty-two.

EUNICE: You don't have to look no further.

BLANCHE (*uncomprehendingly*): I'm looking for my sister, Stella DuBois. I mean – Mrs. Stanley Kowalski.

[handwritten margin note: hasn't / grasped / that she's / married]

EUNICE: That's the party. – You just did miss her, though.

BLANCHE: This – can this be – her home?

EUNICE: She's got the downstairs here and I got the up.

BLANCHE: Oh. She's – out?

EUNICE: You noticed that bowling alley around the corner?

BLANCHE: I'm – not sure I did.

EUNICE: Well, that's where she's at, watchin' her husband bowl. (*There is a pause*.) You want to leave your suitcase here an' go find her?

BLANCHE: No.

NEGRO WOMAN: I'll go tell her you come.

BLANCHE: Thanks.

NEGRO WOMAN: You welcome. (*She goes out*.)

EUNICE: She wasn't expecting you?

BLANCHE: No. No, not tonight.

EUNICE: Well, why don't you just go in and make yourself at home till they get back.

BLANCHE: How could I – do that?

EUNICE: We own this place so I can let you in.

She gets up and opens the downstairs door. A light goes on behind the blind, turning it light blue. BLANCHE *slowly follows her into the downstairs flat. The surrounding areas dim out as the interior is lighted. Two rooms can be seen, not too clearly defined. The one first entered is primarily a kitchen but contains a folding bed to be used by* BLANCHE. *The room beyond this is a bedroom. Off this room is a narrow door to a bathroom.*

EUNICE (*defensively, noticing* BLANCHE's *look*): It's sort of messed up right now but when it's clean it's real sweet.

BLANCHE: Is it?

EUNICE: Uh-huh, I think so. So you're Stella's sister?

BLANCHE: Yes. (*Wanting to get rid of her.*) Thanks for letting me in.

EUNICE: *Por nada*, as the Mexicans say, *por nada*! Stella spoke of you.

BLANCHE: Yes?

EUNICE: I think she said you taught school.

BLANCHE: Yes.

EUNICE: And you're from Mississippi, huh?

BLANCHE: Yes.

EUNICE: She showed me a picture of your home-place, the plantation.

BLANCHE: Belle Reve?

EUNICE: A great big place with white columns.

BLANCHE: Yes . . .

EUNICE: A place like that must be awful hard to keep up.

BLANCHE: If you will excuse me, I'm just about to drop.

EUNICE: Sure, honey. Why don't you set down?

BLANCHE: What I meant was I'd like to be left alone.

EUNICE (*offended*): Aw. I'll make myself scarce, in that case.

BLANCHE: I didn't mean to be rude, but –

EUNICE: I'll drop by the bowling alley an' hustle her up. (*She goes out of the door.*)

BLANCHE *sits in a chair very stiffly with her shoulders slightly hunched and her legs pressed close together and her hands tightly clutching her purse as if she were quite cold. After a while the blind look goes out of her eyes and she begins to look slowly around. A cat screeches. She catches her breath with a startled gesture. Suddenly she notices something in a half opened closet. She springs up and crosses to it, and removes a whisky bottle. She pours a half tumbler of whisky and tosses it down. She carefully replaces the bottle and washes out the tumbler at the sink. Then she resumes her seat in front of the table.*

BLANCHE (*faintly to herself*): I've got to keep hold of myself!

STELLA *comes quickly around the corner of the building and runs to the door of the downstairs flat.*

STELLA (*calling out joyfully*): *Blanche!*

For a moment they stare at each other. Then BLANCHE *springs up and runs to her with a wild cry.*

BLANCHE: Stella, oh, Stella, Stella! Stella for Star!

She begins to speak with feverish vivacity as if she feared for either of them to stop and think. They catch each other in a spasmodic embrace.

BLANCHE: Now, then, let me look at you. But don't you look at me, Stella, no, no, no, not till later, not till I've bathed and rested! And turn that over-light off! Turn that off! I won't be looked at in this merciless glare! (STELLA *laughs and complies*.) Come back here now! Oh, my baby! Stella! Stella for Star! (*She embraces her again*.) I thought you would never come back to this horrible place! What am I saying? I didn't mean to say that. I meant to be nice about it and say – Oh, what a convenient location and such – Ha-a-ah! Precious lamb! You haven't said a *word* to me.

STELLA: You haven't given me a chance to, honey! (*She laughs but her glance at* BLANCHE *is a little anxious*.)

BLANCHE: Well, now you talk. Open your pretty mouth and talk while I look around for some liquor! I know you must have some liquor on the place! Where could it be, I wonder? Oh, I spy, I spy!

She rushes to the closet and removes the bottle; she is shaking all over and panting for breath as she tries to laugh. The bottle nearly slips from her grasp.

STELLA (*noticing*): Blanche, you sit down and let me pour the drinks. I don't know what we've got to mix with. Maybe a coke's in the icebox. Look'n see, honey, while I'm –

BLANCHE: No coke, honey, not with my nerves tonight! Where – where – where is – ?

STELLA: Stanley? Bowling! He loves it. They're having a – found some soda! – tournament . . .

BLANCHE: Just water, baby, to chase it! Now don't get worried, your sister hasn't turned into a drunkard, she's just all shaken up and hot and tired and dirty! You sit down, now, and explain this place to me! What are you

7

doing in a place like this?

STELLA: Now, Blanche –

BLANCHE: Oh, I'm sure not going to be a hypocritical, I'm going to be honestly critical about it! Never, never, never in my worst dreams could I picture – Only Poe! Only Mr Edgar Allan Poe! – could do it justice! Out there I suppose is the ghoul-haunted woodland of Weir! (*She laughs.*)

STELLA: No, honey, those are the L & N tracks.

BLANCHE: No, now seriously, putting joking aside. Why didn't you tell me, why didn't you write me, honey, why didn't you let me know?

STELLA (*carefully, pouring herself a drink*): Tell you what, Blanche?

BLANCHE: Why, that you had to live in these conditions?

STELLA: Aren't you being a little intense about it? It's not that bad at all! New Orleans isn't like other cities.

BLANCHE: This has got nothing to do with New Orleans. You might as well say – forgive me, blessed baby! (*She suddenly stops short.*) The subject is closed!

STELLA (*a little drily*): Thanks.

During the pause, BLANCHE *stares at her. She smiles at* BLANCHE.

BLANCHE (*looking down at her glass, which shakes in her hand*): You're all I've got in the world, and you're not glad to see me!

STELLA (*sincerely*): Why, Blanche, you know that's not true.

BLANCHE: No? – I'd forgotten how quiet you were.

STELLA: You never did give me a chance to say much, Blanche. So I just got in the habit of being quiet around you.

BLANCHE (*vaguely*): A good habit to get into . .
abruptly.) You haven't asked me how I happened to get
away from the school before the spring term ended.

STELLA: Well, I thought you'd volunteer that information –
if you wanted to tell me.

BLANCHE: You thought I'd been fired?

STELLA: No, I – thought you might have – resigned . . .

BLANCHE: I was so exhausted by all I'd been through my –
nerves broke. (*Nervously tamping cigarette*.) I was on the
verge of – lunacy, almost! So Mr Graves – Mr Graves is
the high school superintendent – he suggested I take a
leave of absence. I couldn't put all of those details into
the wire . . . (*She drinks quickly*.) Oh, this buzzes right
through me and feels so *good*!

STELLA: Won't you have another?

BLANCHE: No, one's my limit.

STELLA: Sure?

BLANCHE: You haven't said a word about my appearance.

STELLA: You look just fine.

BLANCHE: God love you for a liar! Daylight never exposed
so total a ruin! But you – you've put on some weight,
yes, you're just as plump as a little partridge! And it's so
becoming to you!

STELLA: No, Blanche –

BLANCHE: Yes, it is, it is or I wouldn't say it! You just have
to watch around the hips a little. Stand up.

STELLA: Not now.

BLANCHE: You hear me? I said stand up! (STELLA *complies
reluctantly*.) You messy child, you, you've spilt something on that pretty white lace collar! About your hair –
you ought to have it cut in a feather bob with your dainty
features. Stella, you have a maid, don't you!

STELLA: No. With only two rooms it's –

9

BLANCHE

STELLA: What? *Two* rooms, did you say?

STELLA: This one and – (*She is embarrassed.*)

BLANCHE: The other one? (*She laughs sharply. There is an embarrassed silence.*) How quiet you are, you're so peaceful. Look how you sit there with your little hands folded like a cherub in choir!

STELLA (*uncomfortably*): I never had anything like your energy, Blanche.

BLANCHE: Well, I never had your beautiful self-control. I am going to take just one little tiny nip more, sort of to put the stopper on, so to speak . . . Then put the bottle away so I won't be tempted. (*She rises.*) I want you to look at *my* figure! (*She turns around.*) You know I haven't put on one ounce in ten years, Stella? I weigh what I weighed the summer you left Belle Reve. The summer Dad died and you left us . . .

STELLA (*a little wearily*): It's just incredible, Blanche, how well you're looking.

BLANCHE: You see I still have that awful vanity about my looks even now that my looks are slipping! (*She laughs nervously and glances at* STELLA *for reassurance.*)

STELLA (*dutifully*): They haven't slipped one particle.

BLANCHE: After all I've been through? You think I believe that story? Blessed child! (*She touches her forehead shakily.*) Stella, there's – only two rooms?

STELLA: And a bathroom.

BLANCHE: Oh, you do have a bathroom! First door to the right at the top of the stairs? (*They both laugh uncomfortably.*) But, Stella, I don't see where you're going to put me!

STELLA: We're going to put you in here.

BLANCHE: What kind of bed's this – one of those collapsible things? (*She sits on it.*)

STELLA: Does it feel all right?

BLANCHE (*dubiously*): Wonderful, honey. I don't like a bed that gives much. But there's no door between the two rooms, and Stanley – <u>will it be decent?</u> *idea put into our heads .? for grandeuria too –*

STELLA: Stanley is Polish, you know.

BLANCHE: Oh, yes. They're something like Irish, aren't they?

STELLA: Well –

BLANCHE: Only not so – highbrow? (*They both laugh again in the same way.*) I brought some nice clothes to meet all your lovely friends in. *anticipating problems*

STELLA: I'm afraid you won't think they are lovely.

BLANCHE: What are they like? *Stella is not blinded by*

STELLA: They're Stanley's friends. *Stanley.*

BLANCHE: Polacks?

STELLA: They're a mixed lot, Blanche.

BLANCHE: Heterogeneous-types?

STELLA: Oh, yes. Yes, types is right!

BLANCHE: Well – anyhow – I brought nice clothes and I'll wear them. I guess you're hoping I'll say I'll put up at a hotel, but I'm not going to put up at a hotel. I want to be *near* you, got to be *with* somebody, I *can't be alone*! Because – as you must have noticed – I'm – *not* very *well* . . . (*Her voice drops and her look is frightened.*)

STELLA: You seem a little nervous or overwrought or something.

BLANCHE: Will Stanley like me, or will I be just a visiting in-law, Stella? I couldn't stand that.

STELLA: You'll get along fine together, if you'll just try not to – well – compare him with men that we went out with at home.

BLANCHE: Is he so – different?

STELLA: Yes. A different species.

11

BLANCHE: In what way; what's he like?

STELLA: Oh, you can't describe someone you're in love with! Here's a picture of him! (*She hands a photograph to* BLANCHE.)

BLANCHE: An officer?

STELLA: A Master Sergeant in the Engineers' Corps. Those are decorations!

BLANCHE: He had those on when you met him?

STELLA: I assure you I wasn't just blinded by all the brass.

BLANCHE: That's not what I –

STELLA: But of course there were things to adjust myself to later on.

BLANCHE: Such as his civilian background! (STELLA *laughs uncertainly*.) How did he take it when you said I was coming?

STELLA: Oh, Stanley doesn't know yet. adds tension

BLANCHE (*frightened*): You – haven't told him?

STELLA: He's on the road a good deal.

BLANCHE: Oh. Travels?

STELLA: Yes.

BLANCHE: Good. I mean – isn't it?

STELLA (*half to herself*): I can hardly stand it when he is away for a night . . .

BLANCHE: Why, Stella?

STELLA: When he's away for a week I nearly go wild!

BLANCHE: Gracious!

STELLA: And when he comes back I cry on his lap like a baby . . . (*She smiles to herself*.)

a lot of passion proves that she is so quiet

BLANCHE: I guess that is what is meant by being in love . . . (STELLA *looks up with a radiant smile*.) Stella –

STELLA: What?

BLANCHE (*in an uneasy rush*): I haven't asked you the things you probably thought I was going to ask. And so I'll

12

expect you to be understanding about what *I* have to tell *you*.

STELLA: What, Blanche? (*Her face turns anxious*.)

BLANCHE: Well, Stella – you're going to reproach me, I know that you're bound to reproach me – but before you do – take into consideration – <u>you left</u>! I stayed and struggled! You came to New Orleans and looked out for yourself! *I* stayed at Belle Reve and tried to hold it together! I'm not meaning this in any reproachful way, but *all* the burden descended on *my* shoulders.

STELLA: The best I could do was make my own living, Blanche.

BLANCHE *begins to shake again with intensity*.

BLANCHE: I know, I know. But you are the one that abandoned Belle Reve, not I! I stayed and fought for it, bled for it, almost died for it!

STELLA: <u>Stop this hysterical outburst and tell me what's happened</u>? What do you mean fought and bled? What kind of –

BLANCHE: I knew you would, Stella. I knew you would take this attitude about it!

STELLA: About – what? – please!

BLANCHE (*slowly*): <u>The loss – the loss</u> . . .

STELLA: Bell Reve? Lost, is it? No!

BLANCHE: Yes, Stella.

They stare at each other across the yellow-checked linoleum of the table. BLANCHE *slowly nods her head and* STELLA *looks slowly down at her hands folded on the table. <u>The music of the "blue piano" grows louder</u>.* BLANCHE *touches her handkerchief to her forehead.*

STELLA: But how did it go? What happened?

13

A Streetcar Named Desire

BLANCHE (*springing up*): You're a fine one to ask me how it
went!

STELLA: Blanche!

BLANCHE: You're a fine one to sit there *accusing me* of it!

STELLA: *Blanche!*

BLANCHE: I, I, *I* took the blows in my face and my body! All
of those deaths! The long parade to the graveyard!
Father, mother! Margaret, that dreadful way! So big
with it, it couldn't be put in a coffin! But had to be
burned like rubbish! You just came home in time for the
funerals, Stella. And funerals are pretty compared to
deaths. Funerals are quiet, but deaths – not always.
Sometimes their breathing is hoarse, and sometimes it
rattles, and sometimes they even cry out to you, "Don't
let me go!" Even the old, sometimes, say, "Don't let me
go." As if you were able to stop them! But funerals are
quiet, with pretty flowers. And, oh, what gorgeous boxes
they pack them away in! Unless you were there at the
bed when they cried out, "Hold me!" you'd never
suspect there was the struggle for breath and bleeding.
You didn't dream, but I saw! *Saw! Saw!* And now you sit
there telling me with your eyes that I let the place go!
How in hell do you think all that sickness and dying was
paid for? Death is expensive, Miss Stella! And old
Cousin Jessie's right after Margaret's, hers! Why, the
Grim Reaper had put up his tent on our doorstep! . . .
Stella. Belle Reve was his headquarters! Honey – that's
how it slipped through my fingers! Which of them left us
a fortune? Which of them left a cent of insurance even?
Only poor Jessie – one hundred to pay for her coffin.
That was all, Stella! And I with my pitiful salary at the
school. Yes, accuse me! Sit there and stare at me,
thinking I let the place go! *I* let the place go? Where

*Blanche; attitude to stanley is being
revealed.*

were *you*. In bed with your – Polack! *jealous*

STELLA (*springing*): Blanche! You be still! That's enough! (*She starts out.*)

BLANCHE: Where are you going?

STELLA: I'm going into the bathroom to wash my face.

BLANCHE: Oh, Stella, Stella, you're crying!

STELLA: Does that surprise you?

STELLA *goes into the bathroom. Outside is the sound of men's voices.* STANLEY, STEVE *and* MITCH *cross to the foot of the steps.*

sudden change in mood

STEVE: And the old lady is on her way to Mass and she's late and there's a cop standin' in front of th' church an' she comes runnin' up an' says, "Officer – is Mass out yet?" He looks her over and says, "No, Lady, but y'r hat's on crooked!" (*They give a hoarse bellow of laughter.*)

STEVE: Playing poker tomorrow night?

STANLEY: Yeah – at Mitch's.

MITCH: Not at my place. My mother's still sick. (*He starts off.*)

STANLEY(*calling after him*): All right, we'll play at my place . . . but you bring the beer.

EUNICE (*hollering down from above*): Break it up down there! I made the spaghetti dish and ate it myself.

STEVE (*going upstairs*): I told you and phoned you we was playing. (*To the men.*) Jax beer!

EUNICE: You never phoned me once.

STEVE: I told you at breakfast – and phoned you at lunch . . .

EUNICE: Well, never mind about that. You just get yourself home here once in a while.

STEVE: You want it in the papers?

15

More laughter and shouts of parting come from the men. STANLEY *throws the screen door of the kitchen open and comes in. He is of medium height, about five feet eight or nine, and strongly, compactly built. Animal joy in his being is implicit in all his movements and attitudes. Since earliest manhood the centre of his life has been pleasure with women, the giving and taking of it, not with weak indulgence, dependently, but with the power and pride of a richly feathered male bird among hens. Branching out from this complete and satisfying centre are all the auxiliary channels of his life, such as his heartiness with men, his appreciation of rough humour, his love of good drink and food and games, his car, his radio, everything that is his, that bears his emblem of the gaudy seed-bearer. He sizes women up at a glance, with sexual classifications, crude images flashing into his mind and determining the way he smiles at them.*

BLANCHE (*drawing involuntarily back from his stare*): You must be Stanley. I'm Blanche.

STANLEY: Stella's sister?

BLANCHE: Yes.

STANLEY: H'lo. Where's the little woman?

BLANCHE: In the bathroom.

STANLEY: Oh. Didn't know you were coming in town.

BLANCHE: I – uh –

STANLEY: Where you from, Blanche?

BLANCHE: Why, I – live in Laurel.

He has crossed to the closet and removed the whisky bottle.

STANLEY: In Laurel, huh? Oh, yeah. Yeah, in Laurel, that's right. Not in my territory. Liquor goes fast in hot weather. (*He holds the bottle to the light to observe its depletion*.) Have a shot?

BLANCHE: No, I – rarely touch it.

STANLEY: Some people rarely touch it, but it touches them often. *He knows that some people are hypocrytical*

BLANCHE (*faintly*): Ha-ha.

STANLEY: My clothes're stickin' to me. Do you mind if I make myself comfortable? (*He starts to remove his shirt*.)

BLANCHE: Please, please do. *showing off. Teasing her?*

STANLEY: Be comfortable is my motto.

BLANCHE: It's mine, too. It's hard to stay looking fresh. I haven't washed or even powdered my face and – here you are!

STANLEY: You know you can catch cold sitting around in damp things, especially when you been exercising hard like bowling is. You're a teacher, aren't you?

BLANCHE: Yes.

STANLEY: What do you teach, Blanche?

BLANCHE: English.

STANLEY: I never was a very good English student. How long you here for, Blanche?

BLANCHE: I – don't know yet.

STANLEY: You going to shack up here?

BLANCHE: I thought I would if it's not inconvenient for you all.

STANLEY: Good.

BLANCHE: Travelling wears me out.

STANLEY: Well, take it easy.

A cat screeches near the window. BLANCHE *springs up*.

BLANCHE: What's that?

STANLEY: Cats . . . Hey, Stella!

STELLA (*faintly, from the bathroom*): Yes, Stanley.

17

STANLEY: Haven't fallen in, have you? (*He grins at* BLANCHE. *She tries unsuccessfully to smile back. There is a silence.*) I'm afraid I'll strike you as being the unrefined type. Stella's spoke of you a good deal. You were married once, weren't you?

The music of the polka rises up, faint in the distance.

BLANCHE: Yes. When I was quite young.
STANLEY: What happened?
BLANCHE: The boy – the boy died. (*She sinks back down.*) I'm afraid I'm – going to be sick!

Her head falls on her arms.

music is symbolic. Haunted by his memory.

SCENE II

It is six o'clock the following evening. BLANCHE *is bathing.*
STELLA is completing her toilette. BLANCHE's *dress, a*
flowered print, is laid out on STELLA's *bed.* STANLEY
enters the kitchen from outside, leaving the door open on
the perpetual "blue piano" around the corner.

STANLEY: What's all this monkey doings?

STELLA: Oh, Stan! (*She jumps up and kisses him which he*
accepts with lordly composure.) I'm taking Blanche to
Galatoires' for supper and then to a show, because it's
your poker night.

STANLEY: How about my supper, huh? I'm not going to no
Galatoire's for supper! *He likes the attention*

STELLA: I put you a cold plate on ice.

STANLEY: Well, isn't that just dandy!

STELLA: I'm going to try to keep Blanche out till the party
breaks up because I don't know how she would take it.
So we'll go to one of the little places in the Quarter
afterwards and you'd better give me some money.

STANLEY: Where is she?

STELLA: She's soaking in a hot tub to quiet her nerves. She's
terribly upset.

STANLEY: Over what?

STELLA: She's been through such an ordeal.

STANLEY: Yeah?

STELLA: Stan, we've – lost Belle Reve!

STANLEY: The place in the country?

STELLA: Yes.

STANLEY: How? *makes it sound like it's not Blanche's fault*

STELLA (*vaguely*): Oh, it had to be – sacrificed or something. (*There is a pause while* STANLEY *considers.* STELLA

implies suffering 19

is changing into her dress.) When she comes in be sure to say something nice about her appearance. And, oh! Don't mention the baby. I haven't said anything yet, I'm waiting until she gets in a quieter condition.

STANLEY (*ominously*): So?

STELLA: And try to understand her and be nice to her, Stan.

BLANCHE (*singing from the bathroom*):

> "From the land of the sky blue water,
>   They brought a captive maid!"

STELLA: She wasn't expecting to find us in such a small place. You see I'd tried to gloss things over a little in my letters. *Stella feels that she has to appologise/*

STANLEY: So? *explain for her sister.*

STELLA: And admire her dress and tell her she's looking wonderful. That's important to Blanche. Her little weakness!

STANLEY: Yeah. I get the idea. Now let's skip back a little to where you said the country place was disposed of.

STELLA: Oh! – yes . . .

STANLEY: How about that? Let's have a few more details on that subject.

STELLA: It's best not to talk much about it until she's calmed down.

STANLEY: So that's the deal, huh? Sister Blanche cannot be annoyed with business details right now!

STELLA: You saw how she was last night.

STANLEY: Uh-hum, I saw how she was. Now let's have a gander at the bill of sale.

STELLA: I haven't seen any.

STANLEY: She didn't show you no papers, no deed of sale or nothing like that, huh?

STELLA: It seems like it wasn't sold.

quite happy to believe B

STANLEY: Well, what in hell was it then, give away? To charity?

STELLA: Shhh! She'll hear you.

STANLEY: I don't care if she hears me. Let's see the papers!

STELLA: There weren't any papers, she didn't show any papers, I don't care about papers.

STANLEY: Have you ever heard of the Napoleonic code?

STELLA: No, Stanley, I haven't heard of the Napoleonic code and if I have, I don't see what it –

STANLEY: Let me enlighten you on a point or two, baby.

STELLA: Yes?

STANLEY: In the state of Louisiana we have the Napoleonic code according to which what belongs to the wife belongs to the husband and vice versa. For instance if I had a piece of property, or you had a piece of property –

STELLA: My head is swimming!

STANLEY: All right. I'll wait till she gets through soaking in a hot tub and then I'll inquire if *she* is acquainted with the Napoleonic code. It looks to me like you have been swindled, baby, and when you're swindled under the Napoleonic code I'm swindled *too*. And I don't like to be *swindled*.

STELLA: There's plenty of time to ask her questions later but if you do now she'll go to pieces again. I don't understand what happened to Belle Reve but you don't know how ridiculous you are being when you suggest that my sister or I or anyone of our family could have perpetrated a swindle on anyone else.

STANLEY: Then where's the money if the place was sold?

STELLA: Not sold – *lost, lost!*

He stalks into bedroom, and she follows him.

STELLA: *Stanley!*

21

He pulls open the wardrobe trunk standing in middle of room and jerks out an armful of dresses.

STANLEY: Open your eyes to this stuff! You think she got them out of a teacher's pay?

STELLA: Hush!

STANLEY: Look at these feathers and furs that she come here to preen herself in! What's this here? A solid-gold dress, I believe! And this one! What is these here? Fox-pieces! (*He blows on them.*) Genuine fox fur-pieces, a half a mile long! Where are your fox-pieces, Stella? Bushy snow-white ones, no less! Where are your white fox-pieces.

STELLA: Those are inexpensive summer furs that Blanche has had a long time.

STANLEY: I got an acquaintance who deals in this sort of merchandise. I'll have him in here to appraise it. I'm willing to bet you there's thousands of dollars invested in this stuff here!

STELLA: Don't be such an idiot, Stanley!

He hurls the furs to the daybed. Then he jerks open small drawer in the trunk and pulls up a fist-full of costume jewellery.

STANLEY: And what have we here? The treasure chest of a pirate!

STELLA: Oh, Stanley!

STANLEY: Pearls! Ropes of them! What is this sister of yours, a deep-sea diver who brings up sunken treasures? Or is she the champion safe-cracker of all time! Bracelets of solid gold, too! Where are your pearls and gold bracelets?

STELLA: Shhh! Be still, Stanley!

STANLEY: And diamonds! A crown for an empress!

STELLA: A rhinestone tiara she wore to a costume ball.

STANLEY: What's rhinestone?

STELLA: Next door to glass.

STANLEY: Are you kidding? I have an acquaintance that works in a jewellery store. I'll have him in here to make an appraisal of this. Here's your plantation, or what was left of it, here!

STELLA: You have no idea how stupid and horrid you're being! Now close that trunk before she comes out of the bathroom!

He kicks the trunk partly closed and sits on the kitchen table.

STANLEY: <u>The Kowalskis and the DuBois have different notions.</u>

STELLA (*angrily*): Indeed they have, thank heavens! – *I'm going outside.* (*She snatches up her white hat and gloves and crosses to the outside door.*) You come out with me while Blanche is getting dressed.

STANLEY: Since when do you give me orders?

STELLA: Are you going to stay and insult her?

STANLEY: You're damn tootin' I'm going to stay here.

STELLA goes out on the porch. BLANCHE comes out of the bathroom in a <u>red satin robe</u>. [Now more relaxed + confident. sexy?]

STANLEY: That's good.

BLANCHE (*drawing the curtains at the windows*): Excuse me while I slip on my pretty new dress!

STANLEY: Go right ahead, Blanche.

She closes the drapes between the rooms.

BLANCHE: I understand there's to be a little card party to

23

which we ladies are cordially *not* invited.

STANLEY (ominously): Yeah?

BLANCHE *throws off her robe and slips into a flowered print dress.*

BLANCHE: Where's Stella?

STANLEY: Out on the porch.

BLANCHE: I'm going to ask a favour of you in a moment.

STANLEY: What could that be, I wonder?

BLANCHE: Some buttons in back! You may enter!

He crosses through drapes with a smouldering look.

BLANCHE: How do I look?

STANLEY: You look all right.

BLANCHE: Many thanks! Now the buttons!

STANLEY: I can't do nothing with them.

BLANCHE: You men with your big clumsy fingers. May I have a drag on your cig?

STANLEY: Have one for yourself.

BLANCHE: Why, thanks! . . . It looks like my trunk has exploded.

STANLEY: Me an' Stella were helping you unpack.

BLANCHE: Well, you certainly did a fast and thorough job of it!

STANLEY: It looks like you raided some stylish shops in Paris.

BLANCHE: Ha-ha! Yes – clothes are my passion!

STANLEY: What does it cost for a string of fur-pieces like that?

BLANCHE: Why, those were a tribute from an admirer of mine!

STANLEY: He must have had a lot of – admiration!

BLANCHE: Oh, in my youth I excited some admiration. But

look at me now! (*She smiles at him radiantly*.) Would you think it possible that I was once considered to be – attractive?

STANLEY: Your looks are okay.

BLANCHE: I was fishing for a compliment, Stanley.

STANLEY: I don't go in for that stuff.

BLANCHE: What – stuff?

STANLEY: Compliments to women about their looks. I never met a woman that didn't know if she was good-looking or not without being told, and some of them give themselves credit for more than they've got. I once went out with a doll who said to me, "I am the glamorous type, I am the glamorous type!" I said, "So what?"

BLANCHE: And what did she say then?

STANLEY: She didn't say nothing. That shut her up like a clam.

BLANCHE: Did it end the romance?

STANLEY: It ended the conversation – that was all. Some men are took in by this Hollywood glamour stuff and some men are not.

BLANCHE: I'm sure you belong in the second category.

STANLEY: That's right.

BLANCHE: I cannot imagine any witch of a woman casting a spell over you. *trying for a star spell over him.*

STANLEY: That's – right.

BLANCHE: You're simple, straightforward and honest, a little bit on the primitive side I should think. To interest you a woman would have to – (*She pauses with an indefinite gesture*.) *Asking him what he wants from her.*

STANLEY (*slowly*): Lay . . . her cards on the table.

BLANCHE (*smiling*): Yes – yes – cards on the table . . . . Well, life is too full of evasions and ambiguities, I think. I like an artist who paints in strong, bold colours, primary

Ironic because that is what her life is like.

25

colours. I don't like pinks and creams and I never cared
for wishy-washy people. That was why, when you
walked in here last night, I said to myself – "My sister
has married a man!" – Of course that was all that I could
tell about you.

STANLEY (*booming*): Now let's cut the re-bop!

BLANCHE (*pressing hand to her ears*): Ouuuuu!

STELLA (*calling from the steps*): Stanley! You come out here
and let Blanche finish dressing!

BLANCHE: I'm through dressing, honey.

STELLA: Well, you come out, then.

STANLEY: Your sister and I are having a little talk.

BLANCHE (*lightly*): Honey, do me a favour. Run to the
drug-store and get me a lemon-coke with plenty of
chipped ice in it! – Will you do that for me, Sweetie?

STELLA (*uncertainly*): Yes. (*She goes around the corner of
the building.*)

BLANCHE: The poor thing was out there listening to us, and
I have an idea she doesn't understand you as well as I do
. . . All right; now, Mr Kowalski, let us proceed without
any more double-talk. I'm ready to answer all questions.
I've nothing to hide. What is it?

STANLEY: There is such a thing in this State of Louisiana as
the Napoleonic code, according to which whatever
belongs to my wife is also mine – and vice versa.

BLANCHE: My, but you have an impressive judicial air!

*She sprays herself with her atomizer; then playfully
sprays him with it. He seizes the atomizer and slams it
down on the dresser. She throws back her head and
laughs.*

STANLEY: If I didn't know that you was my wife's sister I'd
get ideas about you!

26

BLANCHE: Such as what?

STANLEY: Don't play so dumb. You know what! – \
the papers?

BLANCHE: Papers?

STANLEY: Papers! That stuff that people write on!

BLANCHE: Oh, papers, papers! Ha-ha! The first anniversary
gift, all kinds of papers!

STANLEY: I'm talking of legal papers. Connected with the
plantation.

BLANCHE: There *were* some papers.

STANLEY: You mean they're no longer existing?

BLANCHE: They probably are, somewhere.

STANLEY: But not in the trunk.

BLANCHE: Everything I own is in that trunk.

STANLEY: Then why don't we have a look for them? (*He
crosses to the trunk, shoves it roughly open and begins to
open compartments*.) What he wants to do to B.

BLANCHE: What in the name of heaven are you thinking of!
What's in the back of that little boy's mind of yours?
That I am absconding with something, attempting some
kind of treachery on my sister? – Let me do that! It will
be faster and simpler . . . (*She crosses to the trunk and
takes out a box*.) I keep my papers mostly in this tin box.
(*She opens it*.)

STANLEY: What's them underneath? (*He indicates another
sheaf of paper*.)

BLANCHE: These are love-letters, yellowing with antiquity,
all from one boy. (*He snatches them up. She speaks
fiercely*.) Give those back to me!

STANLEY: I'll have a look at them first.

BLANCHE: The touch of your hands insults them!

STANLEY: Don't pull that stuff!

He rips off the ribbon and starts to examine them.

27

BLANCHE *snatches them from him, and they cascade to the floor*.

BLANCHE: Now that you've touched them I'll burn them!

STANLEY (*staring, baffled*): What in hell are they?

BLANCHE (*on the floor gathering them up*): Poems a dead boy wrote. I hurt him the way that you would like to hurt me, but you can't! I'm not young and vulnerable any more. But my young husband was and I – never mind about that! Just give them back to me!

giving out different signals now

STANLEY: What do you mean by saying you'll have to burn them?

BLANCHE: I'm sorry, I must have lost my head for a moment. Everyone has something he won't let others touch because of their – intimate nature . . .

She now seems faint with exhaustion and she sits down with the strong box and puts on a pair of glasses and goes methodically through a large stack of papers.

BLANCHE: Ambler & Ambler. Hmmmmm . . . Crabtree . . . More Ambler & Ambler.

STANLEY: What is Ambler & Ambler?

BLANCHE: A firm that made loans on the place.

STANLEY: Then it *was* lost on a mortgage?

BLANCHE (*touching her forehead*): That must've been what happened.

STANLEY: I don't want no ifs, ands or buts! What's all the rest of them papers?

She hands him the entire box. He carries it to the table and starts to examine the papers.

BLANCHE (*picking up a large envelope containing more papers*): There are thousands of papers, stretching back over hundreds of years, affecting Bell Reve as, piece by piece, our improvident grand-fathers and father and uncles and brothers exchanged the land for their epic fornications – to put it plainly! (*She removes her glasses with an exhausted laugh.*) Till finally all that was left – and Stella can verify that! – was the house itself and about twenty acres of ground, including a graveyard, to which now all but Stella and I have retreated. (*She pours the contents of the envelope on the table.*) Here all of them are, all papers! I hereby endow you with them! Take them, peruse them – commit them to memory, even! I think it's wonderfully fitting that Belle Reve should finally be this bunch of old papers in your big, capable hands! . . . I wonder if Stella's back with my lemon-coke . . .

She leans back and closes her eyes.

STANLEY: I have a lawyer acquaintance who will study these out.

BLANCHE: Present them to him with a box of aspirin tablets.

STANLEY (*becoming somewhat sheepish*): You see, under the Napoleonic code – a man has to take an interest in his wife's affairs – especially now that she's going to have a baby.

BLANCHE *opens her eyes. The "blue piano" sounds louder.*

BLANCHE: Stella? Stella going to have a baby? (*Dreamily.*) I didn't know she was going to have a baby!

She gets up and crosses to the outside door. STELLA *appears around the corner with a carton from the drug-store.* STANLEY *goes into the bedroom with the envelope and the box. The inner rooms fade to darkness and the outside wall of the house is visible.* BLANCHE *meets* STELLA *at the foot of the steps to the sidewalk.*

BLANCHE: Stella, Stella for Star! How lovely to have a baby! (*She embraces her sister.* STELLA *returns the embrace with a convulsive sob.* BLANCHE *speaks softly.*) Everything is all right; we thrashed it out. I feel a bit shaky, but I think I handled it nicely. I laughed and treated it all as a joke, called him a little boy and laughed – and flirted! Yes – I was flirting with your husband, Stella!

STEVE *and* PABLO *appear carrying a case of beer.*

BLANCHE: The guests are gathering for the poker party.

The two men pass between them, and with a short, curious stare at BLANCHE, *they enter the house.*

STELLA: I'm sorry he did that to you.

BLANCHE: He's just not the sort that goes for jasmine perfume! But maybe he's what we need to mix with our blood now that we've lost Belle Reve and have to go on without Belle Reve to protect us . . . How pretty the sky is! I ought to go there on a rocket that never comes down.

A TAMALE VENDOR *calls out as he rounds the corner.*

VENDOR: Red hots! Red hots!

BLANCHE *utters a sharp, frightened cry and shrinks away; then she laughs breathlessly again.*

BLANCHE: Which way do we – go now – Stella?
VENDOR: Re-e-d ho-o-ot!
BLANCHE: The blind are – leading the blind!

They disappear around the corner, BLANCHE'*s desperate laughter ringing out once more. Then there is a bellowing laugh from the interior of the flat. Then the "blue piano" and the hot trumpet sound louder.*

SCENE III

The Poker Night. There is a picture of Van Gogh's of a billiard-parlour at night. The kitchen now suggests that sort of lurid nocturnal brilliance, the raw colours of childhood's spectrum. Over the yellow linoleum of the kitchen table hangs an electric bulb with a vivid green glass shade. The poker players – STANLEY, STEVE, MITCH *and* PABLO *– wear coloured shirts, solid blue, a purple, a red-and-white check, a light green, and they are men at the peak of their physical manhood, as coarse and direct and powerful as the primary colours. there are vivid slices of watermelon on the table, whisky bottles and glasses. The bedroom is relatively dim with only the light that spills between the portières and through the wide window on the street. For a moment there is absorbed silence as a hand is dealt.*

STEVE: Anything wild this deal?

PABLO: One-eyed jacks are wild.

STEVE: Give me two cards.

PABLO: You, Mitch?

MITCH: I'm out.

PABLO: One.

MITCH: Anyone want a shot?

STANLEY: Yeah. Me.

PABLO: Why don't somebody go to the Chinaman's and bring back a load of chop suey?

STANLEY: When I'm losing you want to eat! Ante up! Openers? Openers? Get off the table, Mitch. Nothing belongs on a poker table but cards, chips and whisky.

He lurches up and tosses some watermelon rinds to the floor.

result of drinking
mood building up

31

MITCH: Kind of on your high horse, ain't you?

STANLEY: How many?

STEVE: Give me three.

STANLEY: One.

MITCH: I'm out again. I oughta go home pretty soon.

STANLEY: Shut up.

MITCH: I gotta sick mother. She don't go to sleep until I come in at night. *caring side to M.*

STANLEY: Then why don't you stay home with her?

MITCH: She says to go out, so I go, but I don't enjoy it. All the while I keep wondering how she is.

STANLEY: Aw, for God's sake, go home, then!

PABLO: What've you got?

STEVE: Spade flush.

MITCH: You all are married. But I'll be alone when she goes. – I'm going to the bathroom.

STANLEY: Hurry back and we'll fix you a sugar-tit. *S is rude*

MITCH: Aw, lay off. (*He crosses through the bedroom into the bathroom.*)

STEVE (*dealing a hand*): Seven card stud. (*Telling his joke as he deals.*) This ole nigger is out in back of his house sittin' down th'owing corn to the chickens when all at once he hears a loud cackle and this young hen comes lickety split around the side of the house with the rooster right behind her and gaining on her fast.

STANLEY (*impatient with the story*): Deal! *trying to concentrate*

STEVE: But when the rooster catches sight of the nigger th'owing the corn he puts on the brakes and lets the hen get away and starts pecking corn. And the old nigger says, "Lord God, I hopes I never gits *that* hungry!"

STEVE *and* PABLO *laugh. The sisters appear around the corner of the building.*

32 *timing contrast. Men have been telling sexist jokes + are in that sort of mood*

STELLA: The game is still going on.

BLANCHE: How do I look?

STELLA: Lovely, Blanche.

BLANCHE: I feel so hot and frazzled. Wait till I powder before you open the door. Do I look done in?

STELLA: Why no. You are as fresh as a daisy.

BLANCHE: One that's been picked a few days. *- self knowledge*

STELLA *opens the door and they enter.*

STELLA: Well, well, well. I see you boys are still at it!

STANLEY: Where you been?

STELLA: Blanche and I took in a show. Blanche, this is Mr Gonzales and Mr Hubbel. *- good manners*

BLANCHE: Please don't get up.

STANLEY: Nobody's going to get up, so don't be worried. *very rude*

STELLA: How much longer is this game going to continue?

STANLEY: Till we get ready to quit.

BLANCHE: Poker is so fascinating. Could I kibitz? *B flirting again*

STANLEY: You could not. Why don't you women go up and sit with Eunice?

STELLA: Because it is nearly two-thirty. (BLANCHE *crosses into the bedroom and partially closes the portières.*) Couldn't you call it quits after one more hand?

A chair scrapes. STANLEY *gives a loud whack of his hand on her thigh.* *showing off - He's in control*

STELLA (*sharply*): That's not fun, Stanley.

The men laugh. STELLA *goes into the bedroom.*

STELLA: It makes me so mad when he does that in front of people.

BLANCHE: I think I will bathe. *subconscious desire to be clean*

STELLA: Again? *St↓ S finds it strange*

33

BLANCHE: My nerves are in knots. Is the bathroom occupied?

STELLA: I don't know.

BLANCHE *knocks.* MITCH *opens the door and comes out, still wiping his hands on a towel.*

BLANCHE: Oh! – good evening.

MITCH: Hello. (*He stares at her.*)

STELLA: Blanche, this is Harold Mitchell. My sister, Blanche DuBois.

MITCH (*with awkward courtesy*): How do you do, Miss DuBois.

STELLA: How is your mother now, Mitch?

MITCH: About the same, thanks. She appreciated your sending over that custard. – Excuse me, please.

He crosses slowly back into the kitchen, glancing back at BLANCHE *and coughing a little shyly. He realizes he still has the towel in his hands and with an embarrassed laugh hands it to* STELLA. BLANCHE *looks after him with a certain interest.*

BLANCHE: That one seems – superior to the others.

STELLA: Yes, he is.

BLANCHE: I thought he had a sort of sensitive look.

STELLA: His mother is sick.

BLANCHE: Is he married?

STELLA: No.

BLANCHE: Is he a wolf? someone who preys on women

STELLA: Why, Blanche? (BLANCHE *laughs.*) I don't think he would be.

BLANCHE: What does – what does he do?

She is unbuttoning her blouse.

34 dramatic effect because it is a small place.

STELLA: He's on the precision bench in the spare parts department. At the plant Stanley travels for.

BLANCHE: Is that something much?

STELLA: No. Stanley's the only one of his crowd that's likely to get anywhere. *proud of him .*

BLANCHE: What makes you think Stanley will? *not impressed*

STELLA: Look at him.

BLANCHE: I've looked at him.

STELLA: Then you should know.

BLANCHE: I'm sorry, but I haven't noticed the stamp of genius even on Stanley's forehead.

She takes off the blouse and stands in her pink silk brassière and white skirt in the light through the portières. The game has continued in undertones. *vulnerable*

STELLA: It isn't on his forehead and it isn't genius.

BLANCHE: Oh. Well, what is it, and where? I would like to know.

STELLA: It's a drive that he has. You're standing in the light, Blanche!

BLANCHE: Oh, am I!

She moves out of the yellow streak of light. STELLA *has removed her dress and put on a light blue satin kimono.*

STELLA (*with girlish laughter*): You ought to see their wives.

BLANCHE (*laughingly*): I can imagine. Big, beefy things, I suppose.

STELLA: You know that one upstairs? (*More laughter.*) One time (*laughing*) the plaster – (*laughing*) cracked –

STANLEY: You hens cut out that conversation in there!

STELLA: You can't hear us.

STANLEY: Well, you can hear me and I said to hush up!

STELLA: This is my house and I'll talk as much as I want to!

BLANCHE: Stella, don't start a row.

STELLA: He's half drunk! – I'll be out in a minute.

She goes into the bathroom. BLANCHE *rises and crosses leisurely to a small white radio and turns it on.*

STANLEY: Awright, Mitch, you in?

MITCH: What? Oh! – No, I'm out!

BLANCHE *moves back into the streak of light. She raises her arms and stretches, as she moves indolently back to the chair. Rhumba music comes over the radio.* MITCH *rises at the table.*

Lazy

STANLEY: Who turned that on in there?

BLANCHE: I did. Do you mind?

STANLEY: Turn it off!

STEVE: Aw, let the girls have their music.

PABLO: Sure, that's good, leave it on!

STEVE: Sounds like Xavier Cugat!

STANLEY *jumps up and, crossing to the radio, turns it off. He stops short at sight of* BLANCHE *in the chair. She returns his look without flinching. Then he sits again at the poker table. Two of the men have started arguing hotly.*

STEVE: I didn't hear you name it.

PABLO: Didn't I name it, Mitch?

MITCH: I wasn't listenin'.

PABLO: What were you doing, then?

STANLEY: He was looking through them drapes. (*He jumps up and jerks roughly at curtains to close them.*) Now deal the hand over again and let's play cards or quit. Some people get ants when they win.

MITCH *rises as* STANLEY *returns to his seat.*

STANLEY (*yelling*): Sit down! all getting out of hand.

MITCH: I'm going to the "head". Deal me out.

PABLO: Sure he's got ants now. Seven five-dollar bills in his
   pants pocket folded up tight as spitballs. M doesn't want to lose money now

STEVE: Tomorrow you'll see him at the cashier's window
   getting them changed into quarters. M not big spender.

STANLEY: And when he goes home he'll deposit them one
   by one in a piggy bank his mother give him for making
   Christmas. (*Dealing.*) This game is Spit in the Ocean. fun.
                                                    M outsider?

   MITCH *laughs uncomfortably and continues through
the portières. He stops just inside.*

BLANCHE (*softly*): Hello! The Little Boys' Room is busy
   right now.   euphanism for toilet

MITCH: We've – been drinking beer.

BLANCHE: I hate beer.

MITCH: It's – a hot weather drink.

BLANCHE: Oh, I don't think so; it always makes me warmer.
   Have you got any cigs? (*She has slipped on the dark red
   satin wrapper.*) trying to seduce him

MITCH: Sure.

BLANCHE: What kind are they?

MITCH: Luckies.

BLANCHE: Oh, good. What a pretty case. Silver?

MITCH: Yes. Yes; read the inscription.

BLANCHE: Oh, is there an inscription? I can't make it out.
   (*He strikes a match and moves closer.*) Oh! (*Reading with
   feigned difficulty.*) intimate
      "And if God choose,
         I shall but love thee better – after – death!"
   Why, that's from my favourite sonnet by Mrs Browning!

MITCH: You know it?

BLANCHE: Certainly I do!

MITCH: There's a story connected with that inscription.

BLANCHE: It sounds like a romance.

MITCH: A pretty sad one.

BLANCHE: Oh?

MITCH: The girl's dead now.

BLANCHE (*in a tone of deep sympathy*): *Oh!*

MITCH: She knew she was dying when she give me this. A very strange girl, very sweet – very!

BLANCHE: She must have been fond of you. Sick people have such deep, sincere attachments.

MITCH: That's right, they certainly do.

BLANCHE: Sorrow makes for sincerity, I think.

MITCH: It sure brings it out in people.

BLANCHE: The little there is belongs to people who have experienced some sorrow.

MITCH: I believe you are right about that.

BLANCHE: I'm positive that I am. Show me a person who hasn't known any sorrow and I'll show you a shuperficial – Listen to me! My tongue is a little – thick! You boys are responsible for it. The show let out at eleven and we couldn't come home on account of the poker game so we had to go somewhere and drink. I'm not accustomed to having more than one drink. Two is the limit – and *three*! (*She laughs.*) Tonight I had three. ~~Ms blames it on men~~

STANLEY: Mitch!

MITCH: Deal me out. I'm talking to Miss –

BLANCHE: DuBois.

MITCH: Miss DuBois?

BLANCHE: It's a French name. It means woods and Blanche means white, so the two together mean white woods. Like an orchard in spring! You can remember it by that.

MITCH: You're French.

BLANCHE: We are French by extraction. Our first American ancestors were French Huguenots. *French protestants*

MITCH: You are Stella's sister, are you not?

BLANCHE: Yes, Stella is my precious little sister. I call her little in spite of the fact she's somewhat older than I. Just slightly. Less than a year. Will you do something for me?

MITCH: Sure. What?

BLANCHE: I bought this adorable little coloured paper lantern at a Chinese shop on Bourbon. Put it over the light bulb! Will you, please?

MITCH: Be glad to.

BLANCHE: I can't stand a naked light bulb, any more than I can a rude remark or a vulgar action. *B scared that if people see her in light they will be rude*

MITCH (*adjusting the lantern*): I guess we strike you as being a pretty rough bunch.

BLANCHE: I'm very adaptable – to circumstances.

MITCH: Well, that's a good thing to be. You are visiting Stanley and Stella?

BLANCHE: Stella hasn't been so well lately, and I came down to help her for a while. She's very run down.

MITCH: You're not – ?

BLANCHE: Married? No, no. I'm an old maid schoolteacher!

MITCH: You may teach school but you're certainly not an old maid.

BLANCHE: Thank you, sir! I appreciate your gallantry!

MITCH: So you are in the teaching profession? *upper class, conversation*

BLANCHE: Yes. Ah, yes . . .

MITCH: Grade school or high school or – *St brings them back to earth by shouting. contrast.*

STANLEY (*bellowing*): *Mitch!*

MITCH: *Coming!*

BLANCHE: Gracious, what lung-power . . . I teach high school. In Laurel. *putting down St.*

39

MITCH: What do you teach? What subject?

BLANCHE: Guess!

MITCH: I bet you teach art or music? (BLANCHE *laughs delicately*.) Of course I could be wrong. You might teach arithmetic.

BLANCHE: Never arithmetic, sir; never arithmetic! (*With a laugh*.) I don't even know my multiplication tables! No, I have the misfortune of being an English instructor. I attempt to instil a bunch of bobby-soxers and drug-store Romeos with reverence for Hawthorne and Whitman and Poe!

MITCH: I guess that some of them are more interested in other things. *Sex?*

BLANCHE: How very right you are! Their literary heritage is not what most of them treasure above all else! But they're sweet things! And in the spring, it's touching to notice them making their first discovery of love! As if nobody had ever known it before! *talking about herself.*

The bathroom door opens and STELLA *comes out.* BLANCHE *continues talking to* MITCH.

BLANCHE: Oh! Have you finished? Wait – I'll turn on the radio.

She turns the knobs on the radio and it begins to play "Wien, Wien, nur du allein." BLANCHE *waltzes to the music with romantic gestures.* MITCH *is delighted and moves in awkward imitation like a dancing bear.* STANLEY *stalks fiercely through the portières into the bedroom. He crosses to the small white radio and snatches it off the table. With a shouted oath, he tosses the instrument out of the window.*

STELLA: Drunk – drunk – animal thing, you! (*She rushes*

through to the poker table.) All of you – please go home!
If any of you have one spark of decency in you –
BLANCHE (*wildly*): Stella, watch out, he's –

STANLEY *charges after* STELLA.

MEN (*feebly*): Take it easy, Stanley. Easy fellow. – Let's all
. . .
STELLA: You lay your hands on me and I'll . . .

*She backs out of sight. He advances and disappears.
There is the sound of a blow*. STELLA *cries out.* BLANCHE
*screams and runs into the kitchen. The men rush forward
and there is grappling and cursing. Something is overturned with a crash.*

BLANCHE (*shrilly*): My sister is going to have a baby!
MITCH: This is terrible.
BLANCHE: Lunacy, absolute lunacy!
MITCH: Get him in here men.

STANLEY *is forced, pinioned by the two men, into the
bedroom. He nearly throws them off. Then all at once he
subsides and is limp in their grasp. They speak quietly and
lovingly to him and he leans his face on one of their
shoulders.* St is shocked by what he's done

STELLA (*in a high, unnatural voice, out of sight*): I want to
go away, I want to go away!
MITCH: Poker shouldn't be played in a house with women.

BLANCHE *rushes into the bedroom.*

BLANCHE: I want my sister's clothes! We'll go to that
woman's upstairs!
MITCH: Where is the clothes?
BLANCHE (*opening the closet*): I've got them! (*She rushes*

41

through to STELLA.) Stella, Stella, precious! Dear, dear little sister, don't be afraid!

With her arms around STELLA, BLANCHE *guides her to the outside doors and upstairs.*

STANLEY (*dully*): What's the matter; what's happened?
MITCH: You just blew your top, Stan.
PABLO: He's okay, now.
STEVE: Sure, my boy's okay!
MITCH: Put him on the bed and get a wet towel.
PABLO: I think coffee would do him a world of good, now.
STANLEY (*thickly*): I want water.
MITCH: Put him under the shower!

The men talk quietly as they lead him to the bathroom.

STANLEY: Let go of me, you sons of bitches!

Sounds of blows are heard. The water goes on full tilt.

STEVE: Let's get quick out of here!

They rush to the poker table and sweep up their winnings on their way out.

MITCH (*sadly but firmly*): Poker should not be played in a house with women.

The door closes on them and the place is still. The Negro entertainers in the bar around the corner play "Paper Doll" slow and blue. After a moment STANLEY *comes out of the bathroom dripping water and still in his clinging wet polka dot drawers.*

STANLEY: Stella! (*There is a pause.*) My baby doll's left me!

He breaks into sobs. Then he goes to the phone and dials, still shuddering with sobs.

STANLEY: Eunice? I want my baby! (*He waits a moment; then he hangs up and dials again.*) Eunice! I'll keep on ringin' until I talk with my baby!

An indistinguishable shrill voice is heard. He hurls phone to floor. Dissonant brass and piano sounds as the rooms dim out to darkness and the outer walls appear in the night light. The "blue piano" plays for a brief interval. Finally, STANLEY *stumbles half-dressed out to the porch and down the wooden steps to the pavement before the building. There he throws back his head like a baying hound and bellows his wife's name: "Stella! Stella, sweetheart! Stella!"* Very extreme behaviour

STANLEY: Stell-*lahhhh*!

EUNICE (*calling down from the door of her upper apartment*): Quit that howling out there an' go back to bed!

STANLEY: I want my baby down here. Stella, Stella!

EUNICE: She ain't comin' down so you quit! Or you'll git th' law on you! Enot scared of him. Knows how to treat

STANLEY: Stella! MM

EUNICE: You can't beat on a woman an' then call 'er back! She won't come! And her goin' t' have a baby! . . . You stinker! You whelp of a Polack, you! I hope they do haul you in and turn the fire hose on you, same as the last time!

STANLEY (*humbly*): Eunice, I want my girl to come down with me!

EUNICE: Hah! (*She slams her door.*)

STANLEY (*with heaven-splitting violence*): STELL-LAHHHHHH!

The low-tone clarinet moans. The door upstairs opens again. STELLA *slips down the rickety stairs in her robe. Her eyes are glistening with tears and her hair loose about*

her throat and shoulders. They stare at each other. Then they come together with low, animal moans. He falls to his knees on the steps and presses his face to her belly, curving a little with maternity. Her eyes go blind with tenderness as she catches his head and raises him level with her. He snatches the screen door open and lifts her off her feet and bears her into the dark flat. BLANCHE *comes out on the upper landing in her robe and slips fearfully down the steps.*

BLANCHE: Where is my little sister? Stella? Stella?

She stops before the dark entrance of her sister's flat. Then catches her breath as if struck. She rushes down to the walk before the house. She looks right and left as if for sanctuary. The music fades away. MITCH *appears from around the corner.*

MITCH: Miss DuBois?

BLANCHE: Oh!

MITCH: All quiet on the Potomac now?

BLANCHE: She ran downstairs and went back in there with him.

MITCH: Sure she did.

BLANCHE: I'm terrified!

MITCH: Ho-ho! There's nothing to be scared of. They're crazy about each other.

BLANCHE: I'm not used to such –

MITCH: Naw, it's a shame this had to happen when you just got here. But don't take it serious.

BLANCHE: Violence! Is so –

MITCH: Set down on the steps and have a cigarette with me.

BLANCHE: I'm not properly dressed.

MITCH: That's don't make no difference in the Quarter.

BLANCHE: Such a pretty silver case.

MITCH: I showed you the inscription, didn't I?

BLANCHE: Yes. (*During the pause, she looks up at the sky.*) There's so much – so much confusion in the world . . . (*He coughs diffidently.*) Thank you for being so kind! I need kindness now.

This brings focus back onto B again. Stella goes back to St at the end. she can't help herself. This is a prefiguring of what might happen later.

SCENE IV

It is early the following morning. There is a confusion of street cries like a choral chant. STELLA *is lying down in the bedroom. Her face is serene in the early morning sunlight. One hand rests on her belly, rounding slightly with new maternity. From the other dangles a book of coloured comics. Her eyes and lips have that almost narcotized tranquillity that is in the faces of Eastern idols. The table is sloppy with remains of breakfast and the debris of the preceding night, and* STANLEY's *gaudy pyjamas lie across the threshold of the bathroom. The outside door is slightly ajar on a sky of summer brilliance.* BLANCHE *appears at this door. She has spent a sleepless night and her appearance entirely contrasts with* STELLA's. *She presses her knuckles nervously to her lips as she looks through the door, before entering.*

BLANCHE: Stella?
STELLA (*stirring lazily*): Hmmh? *Contrasts in body movements?*

    BLANCHE *utters a moaning cry and runs into the bedroom, throwing herself down beside* STELLA *in a rush of hysterical tenderness.*

BLANCHE: Baby, my baby sister!
STELLA (*drawing away from her*): Blanche, what is the matter with you?

    BLANCHE *straightens up slowly and stands beside the bed looking down at her sister with knuckles pressed to her lips.*

BLANCHE: He's left?
STELLA: Stan? Yes.

46

Blanche wants stella to leave

BLANCHE: Will he be back?

STELLA: He's gone to get the car greased. Why?

BLANCHE: Why! I've been half crazy, Stella! When I found out you'd been insane enough to come back in here after what happened – I started to rush in after you!

STELLA: I'm glad you didn't.

BLANCHE: What were you thinking of? (STELLA *makes an indefinite gesture*.) Answer me! What? What?

STELLA: Please, Blanche! Sit down and stop yelling.

BLANCHE: All right, Stella. I will repeat the question quietly now. How could you come back in this place last night? Why, you must have slept with him!

STELLA *gets up in a calm and leisurely way.*

STELLA: Blanche, I'd forgotten how excitable you are. You're making much too much fuss about this.

BLANCHE: Am I?

STELLA: Yes, you are, Blanche. I know how it must have seemed to you and I'm awful sorry it had to happen, but it wasn't anything as serious as you seem to take it. In the first place, when men are drinking and playing poker anything can happen. It's always a powder-keg. He didn't know what he was doing . . . He was as good as a lamb when I came back and he's really very, very ashamed of himself.

BLANCHE: And that – that makes it all right?

STELLA: No, it isn't all right for anybody to make such a terrible row, but – people do sometimes. Stanley's always smashed things. Why, on our wedding night – soon as we came in here – he snatched off one of my slippers and rushed about the place smashing the light-bulbs with it.

BLANCHE: He did – *what*?

47

STELLA: He smashed all the light-bulbs with the heel of my slipper! (*She laughs.*)

BLANCHE: And you – you *let* him? Didn't *run*, didn't *scream*? ~~thrilled by his violence~~

STELLA: I was – sort of – thrilled by it. (*She waits for a moment.*) Eunice and you had breakfast?

BLANCHE: Do you suppose I wanted my breakfast?

STELLA: There's some coffee left on the stove.

BLANCHE: You're so – matter of fact about it, Stella.

STELLA: What other can I be? He's taken the radio to get it fixed. It didn't land on the pavement so only one tube was smashed.

BLANCHE: And you are standing there smiling!

STELLA: What do you want me to do?

BLANCHE: Pull yourself together and face the facts.

STELLA: What are they, in your opinion?

BLANCHE: In my opinion? You're married to a madman!

STELLA: No! ~~seeing in Stella something of her own character~~

BLANCHE: Yes, you are, your fix is worse than mine is! Only you're not being sensible about it. I'm going to *do* something. Get hold of myself and make myself a new life!

STELLA: Yes?

BLANCHE: But you've given in. And that isn't right, you're not old! You can get out.

STELLA (*slowly and emphatically*): I'm not in anything I want to get out of.

BLANCHE (*incredulously*): What – Stella?

STELLA: I said I am not in anything that I have a desire to get out of. Look at the mess in this room! And those empty bottles! They went through two cases last night! He promised this morning that he was going to quit having these poker parties, but you know how long such

48

a promise is going to keep. Oh, well, it's his pleasure, like mine is movies and bridge. People have got to tolerate each other's habits, I guess.

BLANCHE: I don't understand you. (STELLA *turns toward her*.) I don't understand your indifference. Is this a Chinese philosophy you've – cultivated?

STELLA: Is what – what?

BLANCHE: This – shuffling about and mumbling – "One tube smashed – beer-bottles – mess in the kitchen" – as if nothing out of the ordinary has happened! (STELLA *laughs uncertainly and picking up the broom, twirls it in her hands*.)

BLANCHE: Are you deliberately shaking that thing in my face.

STELLA: No.

BLANCHE: Stop it. Let go of that broom. I won't have you cleaning up for him!

STELLA: Then who's going to do it? Are you?

BLANCHE: I? I!

STELLA: No, I didn't thinks so.

BLANCHE: Oh, let me think, if only my mind would function! We've got to get hold of some money, that's the way out!

STELLA: I guess that money is always nice to get hold of.

BLANCHE: Listen to me. I have an idea of some kind. (*Shakily she twists a cigarette into her holder*.) Do you remember Shep Huntleigh? (STELLA *shakes her head*.) Of course you remember Shep Huntleigh. I went out with him at college and wore his pin for a while. Well –

STELLA: Well?

BLANCHE: I ran into him last winter. You know I went to Miami during the Christmas holidays?

STELLA: No.

49

desperate + sad

BLANCHE: Well, I did. I took the trip as an investment, thinking I'd meet someone with a million dollars.

STELLA: Did you?

BLANCHE: Yes. I ran into Shep Huntleigh – I ran into him on Biscayne Boulevard, on Christmas Eve, about dusk . . . getting into his car – Cadillac convertible; must have been a block long!

STELLA: I should think it would have been – inconvenient in traffic!

BLANCHE: You've heard of oil-wells?

STELLA: Yes – remotely.

BLANCHE: He has them, all over Texas. Texas is literally spouting gold in his pockets.

STELLA: My, my. *contradiction*

Blosing touch with reality.

BLANCHE: Y'know how indifferent I am to money. I think of money in terms of what it does for you. But he could do it, he could certainly do it!

STELLA: Do what, Blanche?

BLANCHE: Why – set us up in a – shop!

STELLA: What kind of a shop?

BLANCHE: Oh, a – shop of some kind! He could do it with half what his wife throws away at the races.

STELLA: He's married. *B quite jealous person.*

BLANCHE: Honey, would I be here if the man weren't married? (STELLA *laughs a little.* BLANCHE *suddenly springs up and crosses to phone. She speaks shrilly.*) How do I get Western Union? – Operator! Western Union!

STELLA: That's a dial phone, honey. *Not listening to*

BLANCHE: I can't dial, I'm too – *Stella.*

STELLA: Just dial O.

BLANCHE: O?

STELLA: Yes, "O" for Operator! (BLANCHE *considers a moment; then she puts the phone down.*)

BLANCHE: Give me a pencil. Where is a slip of paper? I've got to write it down first – the message, I mean . . .

> *She goes to the dressing-table, and grabs up a sheet of Kleenex and an eyebrow pencil for writing equipment.*

BLANCHE: Let me see now . . . (*She bites the pencil.*) "Darling Shep. Sister and I in desperate situation."
STELLA: I beg your pardon!
BLANCHE: "Sister and I in desperate situation. Will explain details later. Would you be interested in – ?" (*She bites the pencil again.*) "Would you be – interested – in . . . " (*She smashes the pencil on the table and springs up.*) You never get anywhere with direct appeals!
STELLA (*with a laugh*): Don't be so ridiculous, darling!
BLANCHE: But I'll think of something, I've *got* to think of – *some*-thing! Don't, don't laugh at me, Stella! Please, please don't – I – I want you to look at the contents of my purse! Here's what's in it! (*She snatches her purse open.*) Sixty-five measly cents in coin of the realm!
STELLA (*crossing to bureau*): Stanley doesn't give me a regular allowance, he likes to pay bills himself, but – this morning he gave me ten dollars to smooth things over. You take five of it, Blanche, and I'll keep the rest.
BLANCHE: Oh, no. No, Stella.
STELLA (*insisting*): I know how it helps your morale just having a little pocket-money on you.
BLANCHE: No, thank you – I'll take to the streets!
STELLA: Talk sense! How did you happen to get so low on funds?
BLANCHE: Money just goes – it goes places. (*She rubs her forehead.*) Sometime today I've got to get hold of a bromo!
STELLA: I'll fix you one now.

51

BLANCHE: Not yet – I've got to keep thinking!

STELLA: I wish you'd just let things go, at least for a – while

[handwritten: She needed security.]

BLANCHE: Stella, I can't live with him! You can, he's your husband. But how could I stay here with him, after last night, with just those curtains between us?

[handwritten margin: very aware of his sexuality]

STELLA: Blanche, you saw him at his worst last night.

BLANCHE: On the contrary, I saw him at his best! What such a man has to offer is animal force and he gave a wonderful exhibition of that! But the only way to live with such a man is to – go to bed with him! And that's your job – not mine!

[handwritten margin: B finds his violence attractive too.]

STELLA: After you've rested a little, you'll see it's going to work out. You don't have to worry about anything while you're here. I mean – expenses . . .

BLANCHE: I have to plan for us both, to get us both – out!

STELLA: You take it for granted that I am in something that I want to get out of.

BLANCHE: I take it for granted that you still have sufficient memory of Belle Reve to find this place and these poker players impossible to live with.

STELLA: Well, you're taking entirely too much for granted.

BLANCHE: I can't believe you're in earnest.

STELLA: No?

BLANCHE: I understand how it happened – a little. You saw him in uniform, an officer, not here but –

STELLA: I'm not sure it would have made any difference where I saw him.

BLANCHE: Now don't say it was one of those mysterious electric things between people! If you do I'll laugh in your face. *[handwritten: Relies. Wants what they've got]*

STELLA: I am not going to say anything more at all about it!

BLANCHE: All right, then, don't!

STELLA: But there are things that happen between a man and a woman in the dark – that sort of make everything else seem – unimportant. (*Pause.*) [This is what she feels, but is horrible to Stella about it.]

BLANCHE: What are you talking about is brutal desire – just – Desire! – the name of that rattle-trap street-car that bangs through the Quarter, up one old narrow street and down another . . .

STELLA: Haven't you ever ridden on that street-car? [ie – haven't you ever felt that way?]

BLANCHE: It brought me here. – Where I'm not wanted and where I'm ashamed to be . . . [double meaning. trapped by this desire in Oreal, so came to Stella & Stanley]

STELLA: Then don't you think your superior attitude is a bit out of place? [change of mood now.]

BLANCHE: I am not being or feeling at all superior, Stella. Believe me I'm not! It's just this. This is how I look at it. A man like that is someone to go out with – once – twice – three times when the devil is in you. But live with! Have a child by?

STELLA: I have told you I love him.

BLANCHE: Then I *tremble* for you! I just – *tremble* for you . . .

STELLA: I can't help your trembling if you insist on trembling!

There is a pause.

BLANCHE: May I – speak – *plainly*?

STELLA: Yes, do. Go ahead. As plainly as you want to.

Outside, a train approaches. They are silent till the noise subsides. They are both in the bedroom. Under cover of the train's noise STANLEY *enters from outside. He stands unseen by the women, holding some packages in his arms, and overhears their following conversation. He wears an undershirt and grease-stained seersucker pants.*

BLANCHE: Well – if you'll forgive me – he's *common*!

STELLA: Why, yes, I suppose he is.

BLANCHE: Suppose! You can't have forgotten that much of our bringing up, Stella, that you just *suppose* that any part of a gentleman's in his nature! *Not one particle, no!* Oh, if he was just – *ordinary*! Just *plain* – but good and wholesome, but – *no*. There's something downright – *bestial* – about him! You're hating me saying this, aren't you?

STELLA (*coldly*): Go on and say it all, Blanche.

BLANCHE: He acts like an animal, has an animal's habits! Eats like one, moves like one, talks like one! There's even something – sub-human – something not quite to the stage of humanity yet! Yes, something – ape-like about him, like one of those pictures I've seen in – anthropological studies! Thousands and thousands of years have passed him right by, and there he is – Stanley Kowalski – survivor of the stone age! Bearing the raw meat home from the kill in the jungle! And you – *you* here – *waiting* for him! Maybe he'll strike you or maybe grunt and kiss you! That is, if kisses have been discovered yet! Night falls and the other apes gather! There in the front of the cave, all grunting like him, and swilling and gnawing and hulking! His poker night! – you call it – this party of apes! Somebody growls – some creature snatches at something – the fight is on! *God!* Maybe we are a long way from being made in God's image, but Stella – my sister – there has been *some* progress since then! Such things as art – as poetry and music – such kinds of new light have come into the world since then! In some kinds of people some tenderer feelings have had some little beginning! That we have got to make *grow*! And *cling* to, and hold as our flag! In

54

this dark march toward whatever it is we're approa . . . *Don't – don't hang back with the brutes!*

Another train passes outside. STANLEY *hesitates, licking his lips. Then suddenly he turns stealthily about and withdraws through front door. The women are still unaware of his presence. When the train has passed he calls through the closed front door.*

STANLEY: Hey! Hey, Stella!
STELLA (*who has listened gravely to* BLANCHE): Stanley!
BLANCHE: Stell, I –

But STELLA *has gone to the front door.* STANLEY *enters casually with his packages.*

STANLEY: Hiyuh, Stella, Blanche back?
STELLA: Yes, she's back.
STANLEY: Hiyuh, Blanche. (*He grins at her.*) Usually rude to her

STELLA: You must've got under the car.
STANLEY: Them darn mechanics at Fritz's don't know their can from third base!

STELLA *has embraced him with both arms, fiercely, and full in the view of* BLANCHE. *He laughs and clasps her head to him. Over her head he grins through the curtains at* BLANCHE. *As the lights fade away, with a lingering brightness on their embrace, the music of the "blue piano" and trumpet and drums is heard.*

S is under st. power, not B.

SCENE V

BLANCHE *is seated in the bedroom fanning herself with a palm leaf as she reads over a just completed letter. Suddenly she bursts into a peal of laughter.* STELLA *is dressing in the bedroom.*

STELLA: What are you laughing at, honey?

BLANCHE: Myself, myself, for being such a liar! I'm writing a letter to Shep. (*She picks up the letter.*) "Darling Shep. I am spending the summer on the wing, making flying visits here and there. And who knows, perhaps I shall take a sudden notion to *swoop* down on *Dallas*! How would you feel about that? Ha-ha! (*She laughs nervously and brightly, touching her throat as if actually talking to* SHEP.) Forewarned is forearmed, as they say!" – How does that sound?

STELLA: Uh-huh . . .

BLANCHE (*going on nervously*): "Most of my sister's friends go north in the summer but some have homes on the Gulf and there has been a continued round of entertainments, teas, cocktails, and luncheons – "

A disturbance is heard upstairs at the HUBBELS' *apartment.*

STELLA (*crossing to the door*): Eunice seems to be having some trouble with Steve.

EUNICE'S *voice shouts in terrible wrath.*

EUNICE: I heard about you and that blonde!

STEVE: That's a damn lie!

EUNICE: You ain't pulling the wool over my eyes! I wouldn't

56

mind if you'd stay down at the Four Deuces, but you always going up.

STEVE: Who ever seen me up?

EUNICE: I seen you chasing her 'round the balcony – I'm gonna call the vice squad!

STEVE: Don't you throw that at me!

EUNICE (*shrieking*): You hit me! I'm gonna call the police!

A clatter of aluminium striking a wall is heard, followed by a man's angry roar, shouts and overturned furniture. There is a crash; then a relative hush.

BLANCHE (*brightly*): Did he *kill* her? *[handwritten: "cannot get used to what's going on. S treats it like everyday life"]*

EUNICE *appears on the steps in daemonic disorder.*

STELLA: No! She's coming downstairs.

EUNICE: Call the police, I'm going to call the police! (*She rushes around the corner.*)

STELLA (*returning from the door*): Some of your sister's friends have stayed in the city. *[handwritten: "My comment. B & S laughing together at others"]*

They laugh lightly. STANLEY *comes around the corner in his green and scarlet silk bowling shirt. He trots up the steps and bangs into the kitchen.* BLANCHE *registers his entrance with nervous gestures.*

STANLEY: What's a matter with Eun-uss?

STELLA: She and Steve had a row. Has she got the police?

STANLEY: Naw. She's gettin' a drink.

STELLA: That's much more practical!

STEVE *comes down nursing a bruise on his forehead and looks in the door.*

STEVE: *She here*?

STANLEY: Naw, naw. At the Four Deuces.

STEVE: That hunk! (*He looks around the corner a bit*

timidly, then turns with affected boldness and runs after her.)

BLANCHE: I must jot that down in my notebook. Ha-ha! I'm compiling a notebook of quaint little words and phrases I've picked up here.

STANLEY: You won't pick up nothing here you ain't heard before.

BLANCHE: Can I count on that?

STANLEY: You can count on it up to five hundred.

BLANCHE: That's a mighty high number. (*He jerks open the bureau drawer, slams it shut and throws shoes in a corner. At each noise* BLANCHE *winces slightly. Finally she speaks.*) What sign were you born under?

STANLEY (*while he is dressing*): Sign?

BLANCHE: Astrological sign. I bet you were born under Aries. Aries people are forceful and dynamic. They dote on noise! They love to bang things around! You must have had lots of banging around in the army, and now that you're out, you make up for it by treating inanimate objects with such a fury!

STELLA *has been going in and out of the closet during this scene. Now she pops her head out of the closet.*

STELLA: Stanley was born just five minutes after Christmas.

BLANCHE: Capricorn – the Goat!

STANLEY: What sign were *you* born under?

BLANCHE: Oh, my birthday's next month, the fifteenth of September; that's under Virgo.

STANLEY: What's Virgo.

BLANCHE: Virgo is the Virgin.

STANLEY (*contemptuously*): *Hah*! (*He advances a little as he knots his tie.*) Say, do you happen to know somebody named Shaw!

58

Her face expresses a faint shock. She reaches for the cologne bottle and dampens her handkerchief as she answers carefully. trying to make herself smell sweet

BLANCHE: Why, everybody knows somebody named Shaw!

STANLEY: Well, this somebody named Shaw is under the impression he met you in Laurel, but I figure he must have got you mixed up with some other party because this other party is someone he met at a hotel called the Flamingo.

Perfume being used as a symbol.

BLANCHE laughs breathlessly as she touches the cologne-dampened handkerchief to her temples.

BLANCHE: I'm afraid he does have me mixed up with this "other party". The Hotel Flamingo is not the sort of establishment I would dare to be seen in!

STANLEY: You know of it?

BLANCHE: Yes, I've seen it and smelled it.

STANLEY: You must've got pretty close if you could smell it.

BLANCHE: The odour of cheap perfume is penetrating.

STANLEY: That stuff you use is expensive? Questioning her standing & morals.

BLANCHE: Twenty-five dollars an ounce! I'm nearly out. & knows That's just a hint if you want to remember my birthday! what he means but (*She speaks lightly but her voice has a note of fear.*) tries to keep

STANLEY: Shaw must've got you mixed up. He goes in and it light out of Laurel all the time, so he can check on it and clear Flirtation up any mistake. Talking is her self defence.

He turns away and crosses to the portières. BLANCHE *closes her eyes as if faint. Her hand trembles as she lifts the handkerchief again to her forehead.* STEVE *and* EUNICE *come around corner.* STEVE's *arm is around* EUNICE's *shoulder and she is sobbing luxuriously and he is cooing love-words. There is a murmur of thunder as*

E is completely opposite to B. E has open notions. B's are inside. B might feel like being but she can't

59

they go slowly upstairs in a tight embrace.

STANLEY (*to* STELLA): I'll wait for you at the Four Deuces!

STELLA: Hey! Don't I rate one kiss?

STANLEY: Not in front of your sister.

He goes out. BLANCHE *rises from her chair. She seems faint; looks about her with an expression of almost panic.*

BLANCHE: Stella! What have you heard about me?

STELLA: Huh?

BLANCHE: What have people been telling you about me?

STELLA: Telling?

BLANCHE: You haven't heard any – unkind – gossip about me?

STELLA: Why, no, Blanche, of course not!

BLANCHE: Honey, there was – a good deal of talk in Laurel.

STELLA: About *you*, Blanche?

STELLA: I wasn't so good the last two years or so, after Belle Reve had started to slip through my fingers.

STELLA: All of us do things we –

BLANCHE: I never was hard or self-sufficient enough. When people are soft – soft people have got to court the favour of hard ones, Stella. Have got to be seductive – put on soft colours, the colours of butterfly wings, and glow – make a little – temporary magic just in order to pay for – one night's shelter! That's why I've been – not so awf'ly good lately. I've run for protection, Stella, from under one leaky roof to another leaky roof – because it was storm – all storm, and I was – caught in the centre . . . People don't see you – *men* don't – don't even admit your existence unless they are making love to you. And you've got to have your existence admitted by someone, if you're going to have someone's protection. And so the soft people have got to – shimmer and glow – put a –

60

paper lantern over the light . . . But I'm scared now –
awf'ly scared. I don't know how much longer I can turn
the trick. It isn't enough to be soft. You've got to be soft
and attractive. And I – I'm fading now!

The afternoon has faded to dusk. STELLA *goes into the
bedroom and turns on the light under the paper lantern.
She holds a bottled soft drink in her hand.*

BLANCHE: Have you been listening to me?
STELLA: I don't listen to you when you are being morbid!
   (*She advances with the bottled coke.*)
BLANCHE (*with abrupt change to gaiety*): Is that coke for
   me?
STELLA: Not for anyone else!
BLANCHE: Why, you precious thing, you! Is it just coke?
STELLA (*turning*): You mean you want a shot in it!
BLANCHE: Well, honey, a shot never does a coke any harm!
   Let me? You mustn't wait on me!
STELLA: I like to wait on you, Blanche. It makes it seem
   more like home. (*She goes into the kitchen, finds a glass
   and pours a shot of whisky into it.*)
BLANCHE: I have to admit I love to be waited on . . .

She rushes into the bedroom. STELLA *goes to her with
the glass.* BLANCHE *suddenly clutches* STELLA's *free hand
with a moaning sound and presses the hand to her lips.*
STELLA *is embarrassed by her show of emotion.* BLANCHE
speaks in a choked voice.

BLANCHE: You're – you're – so *good* to me! And I –
STELLA: Blanche.
BLANCHE: I know, I won't! You hate me to talk sentimen-
   tal. But honey, *believe* I feel things more than I *tell* you! I
   won't stay long! I won't, I *promise* I –

61

STELLA: Blanche!

BLANCHE (*hysterically*): I won't, I promise, *I'll go! Go soon!* I will *really*! I *won't* hang around until he – throws me out . . .

STELLA: Now will you stop talking foolish?

BLANCHE: Yes, honey. Watch how you pour – that fizzy stuff foams over!

> BLANCHE *laughs shrilly and grabs the glass, but her hand shakes so it almost slips from her grasp.* STELLA *pours the coke into the glass. It foams over and spills.* BLANCHE *gives a piercing cry.*

STELLA (*shocked by the cry*): Heavens!

BLANCHE: Right on my pretty white skirt!

STELLA: Oh . . . Use my hanky. Blot gently.

BLANCHE (*slowly recovering*): I know – gently – gently . . .

STELLA: Did it stain?

BLANCHE: Not a bit. Ha-ha! Isn't that lucky? (*She sits down shakily, taking a grateful drink. She holds the glass in both hands and continues to laugh a little.*)

STELLA: Why did you scream like that?

BLANCHE: I don't know why I scream! (*Continuing nervously.*) Mitch – Mitch is coming at seven. I guess I am just feeling nervous about our relations. (*She begins to talk rapidly and breathlessly.*) He hasn't gotten a thing but a thing but a goodnight kiss, that's all I have given him, Stella. I want his respect. And men don't want anything they get too easy. But on the other hand men lose interest quickly. Especially when the girl is over – thirty. They think a girl over thirty ought to – the vulgar term is – "put out." . . . And I – I'm not "putting out." Of course he – he doesn't know – I mean I haven't informed him – of my real age!

62

STELLA: Why are you sensitive about your age?

BLANCHE: Because of hard knocks my vanity's been given.
What I mean is – he thinks I'm sort of – prim and proper,
you know! (*She laughs out sharply.*) I want to *deceive*
him enough to make him – want me . . . *Blas low esteem*

STELLA: Blanche, do you want *him*? *She's getting honest*

BLANCHE: I want to *rest*! I want to breathe quietly again!
Yes – I *want* Mitch . . . *very badly*! Just think! If it
happens! I can leave here and not be anyone's problem
. . . *She wants security after everything that has happened*

STANLEY *comes around the corner with a drink under
his belt.* *Blanche is always interrupted*

STANLEY (*bawling*): Hey, Steve! Hey, Eunice! Hey, Stella!

*There are joyous calls from above. Trumpet and drums
are heard from around the corner.*

STELLA (*kissing* BLANCHE *impulsively*): It *will* happen!

BLANCHE (*doubtfully*): It will?

STELLA: It *will*! (*She goes across into the kitchen, looking
back at* BLANCHE.) It will, honey, *it will* . . . But don't
take another drink! (*Her voice catches as she goes out of
the door to meet her husband.*)

BLANCHE *sinks faintly back in her chair with her drink.*
EUNICE *shrieks with laughter and runs down the steps.*
STEVE *bounds after her with goat-like screeches and
chases her around corner.* STANLEY *and* STELLA *twine
arms as they follow, laughing. Dusk settles deeper. The
music from the Four Deuces is slow and blue.* *This might
explain the mood she is in when young man comes*

BLANCHE: Ah, me, ah, me, ah, me . . .

Her eyes fall shut and the palm leaf drops from her

fingers. She slaps her hand on the chair arm a couple of times; then she raises herself wearily to her feet and picks up the hand mirror. There is a little glimmer of lightning about the building. The NEGRO WOMAN, *cackling hysterically, swaying drunkenly, comes around the corner from the Four Deuces. At the same time, a* YOUNG MAN *enters from the opposite direction. The* NEGRO WOMAN *snaps her fingers before his belt.*

NEGRO WOMAN: Hey! Sugar!

She says something indistinguishable. The YOUNG MAN *shakes his head violently and edges hastily up the steps. He rings the bell.* BLANCHE *puts down the mirror. The* NEGRO WOMAN *has wandered down the street.*

BLANCHE: Come in.

The YOUNG MAN *appears through the portières. She regards him with interest.*

BLANCHE: Well, well! What can I do for *you*?

YOUNG MAN: I'm collecting for *The Evening Star*.

BLANCHE: I didn't know that stars took up collections.

YOUNG MAN: It's the paper.

BLANCHE: I know, I was joking – feebly! Will you – have a drink?

YOUNG MAN: No, ma'am. No, thank you. I can't drink on the job.

BLANCHE: Oh, well, now, let's see . . . No, I don't have a dime! I'm not the lady of the house. I'm her sister from Mississippi. I'm one of those poor relations you've heard about.

YOUNG MAN: That's all right. I'll drop by later. (*He starts to go out. She approaches a little.*)

BLANCHE: Hey! (*He turns back shyly. She puts a cigarette in a long holder.*) Could you give me a light? (*She crosses toward him. They meet at the door between the two rooms.*)

YOUNG MAN: Sure. (*He takes out a lighter.*) This doesn't always work. *talking about herself, perhaps. Usual chat up*

BLANCHE: It's temperamental? (*It flares.*) Ah! thank you. *- line*

YOUNG MAN: Thank *you*! (*He starts away again.*)

BLANCHE: Hey! (*He turns again, still more uncertainly. She goes close to him.*) What time is it?

DOCTOR: Fifteen of seven.

BLANCHE: So late? Don't you just love these long rainy afternoons in New Orleans when an hour isn't just an hour – but a little bit of Eternity dropped in your hands – and who knows what to do with it? *She doesn't really like them.*

YOUNG MAN: Yes, ma'am. *She can't handle being alone. She has to be with somebody.*

In the ensuing pause, the "blue piano" is heard. It continues through the rest of this scene and the opening of the next. The YOUNG MAN *clears his throat and looks glancingly at the door.* *B is v. desperate*

BLANCHE: You – uh – didn't get wet in the shower?

YOUNG MAN: No, ma'am. I stepped inside.

BLANCHE: In a drug-store? And had a soda?

YOUNG MAN: Uhhuh.

BLANCHE: Chocolate?

YOUNG MAN: No, ma'am. Cherry. *- losing virginity?*

BLANCHE: Mmmm! *- That's why she likes it.*

YOUNG MAN: A cherry soda! *innocent/naive (symbol)*

BLANCHE: You make my mouth water.

YOUNG MAN: Well, I'd better be –

BLANCHE: Young man! Young, young, young, young – man! Has anyone ever told you that you look like a young prince out of the Arabian Nights? *makes her seem drunk. seems like whole thing is slipping.*

Her age is a problem.

YOUNG MAN: No, ma'am.

> *The* YOUNG MAN *laughs uncomfortably and stands like a bashful kid.* BLANCHE *speaks softly to him.*

BLANCHE: Well, you do, honey lamb. Come here! Come on over here like I told you! I want to kiss you – just once – softly and sweetly on your mouth. (*Without waiting for him to accept, she crosses quickly to him and presses her lips to his.*) Run along now! It would be nice to keep you, but I've got to be good and keep my hands off children. Adios! *referring to the past*

YOUNG MAN: Huh?

> *He stares at her a moment. She opens the door for him and blows a kiss to him as he goes down the steps with a dazed look. She stands there a little dreamily after he has disappeared. Then* MITCH *appears around the corner with a bunch of roses.*

She's been in a fantasy land for just one moment

Irony is that M is real and she can't handle reality either.

BLANCHE: Look who's coming! My Rosenkavalier! Bow to me first! Now present them. *dominating him. Seems like a bit of fun.*

> *He does so. She curtsies low.*

BLANCHE: Ahhh! Merciii!

66

SCENE VI

It is about two a.m. the same night. The outer wall of the building is visible. BLANCHE *and* MITCH *come in. The utter exhaustion which only a neurasthenic personality can know is evident in* BLANCHE's *voice and manner.* MITCH *is solid but depressed. They have probably been out to the amusement park on Lake Pontchartrain, for* MITCH *is bearing, upside down, a plaster statuette of Mae West, the sort of prize won at shooting-galleries and carnival games of chance.*

BLANCHE (*stopping lifelessly at the steps*): Well . . .

    MITCH *laughs uneasily.*

BLANCHE: Well . . .

MITCH: I guess it must be pretty late – and you're tired.

BLANCHE: Even the hot tamale man has deserted the street, and he hangs on till the end. (MITCH *laughs uneasily again.*) How will you get home?

MITCH: I'll walk over to Bourbon and catch an owl-car.

BLANCHE (*laughing grimly*): Is that street-car named Desire still grinding along the tracks at this hour?

MITCH (*heavily*): I'm afraid you haven't gotten much fun out of this evening, Blanche.

BLANCHE: I spoiled it for *you*.

MITCH: No, you didn't, but I felt all the time that I wasn't giving you much – entertainment.

BLANCHE: I simply couldn't rise to the occasion. That was all. I don't think I've ever tried to be gay and made such a dismal mess of it. I get ten points for trying – I *did* try.

MITCH: Why did you try if you didn't feel like it, Blanche?

BLANCHE: I was just obeying the law of nature.

67

MITCH: Which law is that?

BLANCHE: The one that says the lady must entertain the gentleman – or no dice! See if you can locate my door-key in this purse. When I'm so tired my fingers are all thumbs!

MITCH (*rooting in her purse*): This it?

BLANCHE: No, honey, that's the key to my trunk which I must soon be packing.

MITCH: You mean you are leaving here soon?

BLANCHE: I've outstayed my welcome.

MITCH: This it?

The music fades away.

BLANCHE: Eureka! Honey, you open the door while I take a last look at the sky. (*She leans on the porch rail. He opens the door and stands awkwardly behind her.*) I'm looking for the Pleiades, the Seven Sisters, but these girls are not out tonight. Oh, yes they are, there they are! God bless them! All in a bunch going home from their little bridge party . . . Y' get the door open? Good boy! I guess you – want to go now . . .

He shuffles and coughs a little.

MITCH: Can I – uh – kiss you – good night?

BLANCHE: Why do you always ask me if you may?

MITCH: I don't know whether you want me to or not.

BLANCHE: Why should you be so doubtful?

MITCH: That night when we parked by the lake and I kissed you, you –

BLANCHE: Honey, it wasn't the kiss I objected to. I liked the kiss very much. It was the other little – familiarity – that I – felt obliged to – discourage . . . I didn't resent it! Not a bit in the world! In fact, I was somewhat flattered that you – desired me! But, honey, you know as well as I do that a single girl, a girl alone in the world, has got to keep a firm hold on her emotions or she'll be lost!

MITCH (*solemnly*): Lost?

BLANCHE: I guess you are used to girls that like to be lost. The kind that get lost immediately, on the first date!

MITCH: I like you to be exactly the way that you are, because in all my – experience – I have never known anyone like you.

BLANCHE *looks at him gravely; then she bursts into laughter and then claps a hand to her mouth.*

MITCH: Are you laughing at me?

BLANCHE: No, honey. The lord and lady of the house have not yet returned, so come in. We'll have a night-cap. Let's leave the lights off. Shall we?

MITCH: You just – do what you want to.

BLANCHE *precedes him into the kitchen. The outer wall of the building disappears and the interiors of the two rooms can be dimly seen.*

BLANCHE (*remaining in the first room*): The other room's more comfortable – go on in. This crashing around in the dark is my search for some liquor.

MITCH: You want a drink?

BLANCHE: I want *you* to have a drink! You have been so anxious and solemn all evening, and so have I; we have both been anxious and solemn and now for these few last remaining moments of our lives together – I want to create – *joie de vivre*! I'm lighting a candle.

MITCH: That's good.

BLANCHE: We are going to be very Bohemian. We are going to pretend that we are sitting in a little artists' cafe on the

69

Left Bank in Paris! (*She lights a candle stub and puts it in a bottle*.) *Je Suis la Dame aux Camellias! Vous êtes – Armand!* Understand French?

MITCH (*heavily*): Naw. Naw, I –

BLANCHE: *Voulez-vous couchez avec moi ce soir? Vous ne comprenez pas? Ah, quel dommage!* – I mean it's a damned good thing . . . I've found some liquor! Just enough for two shots without any dividends, honey . . .

MITCH (*heavily*): That's – good.

She enters the bedroom with the drinks and the candle.

BLANCHE: Sit down! Why don't you take off your coat and loosen your collar!

MITCH: I better leave it on.

BLANCHE: No. I want you to be comfortable.

MITCH: I am ashamed of the way I perspire. My shirt is sticking to me.

BLANCHE: Perspiration is healthy. If people didn't perspire they would die in five minutes. (*She takes his coat from him.*) This is a nice coat. What kind of material is it?

MITCH: They call that stuff alpaca.

BLANCHE: Oh. Alpaca.

MITCH: It's very light weight alpaca.

BLANCHE: Oh. Light weight alpaca.

MITCH: I don't like to wear a wash-coat even in summer because I sweat through it.

BLANCHE: Oh.

MITCH: And it don't look neat to me. A man with a heavy build has got to be careful of what he puts on him so he don't look too clumsy.

BLANCHE: You are not too heavy.

MITCH: You don't think I am?

BLANCHE: You are not the delicate type. You have a

70

massive bone-structure and a very imposing physique.

MITCH: Thank you. Last Christmas I was given a member-
ship to the New Orleans Athletic Club.

BLANCHE: Oh, good.

MITCH: It was the finest present I ever was given. I work out
there with the weights and I swim and I keep myself fit.
When I started there, I was getting soft in the belly but
now my belly is hard. It is so hard that now a man can
punch me in the belly and it don't hurt me. Punch me!
Go on! See? (*She pokes lightly at him.*)

BLANCHE: Gracious. (*Her hand touches her chest.*)

MITCH: Guess how much I weigh, Blanche?

BLANCHE: Oh, I'd say in the vicinity of – one hundred and
eighty?

MITCH: Guess again.

BLANCHE: Not that much?

MITCH: No. More.

BLANCHE: Well, you're a tall man and you can carry a good
deal of weight without looking awkward.

MITCH: I weigh two hundred and seventy pounds and I'm six
feet one and one half inches tall in my bare feet – without
shoes on. And that is what I weigh stripped.

BLANCHE: Oh, my goodness, me! It's awe-inspiring.

MITCH (*embarrassed*): My weight is not a very interesting
subject to talk about. (*He hesitates for a moment.*)
What's yours?

BLANCHE: My weight?

MITCH: Yes.

BLANCHE: Guess!

MITCH: Let me lift you.

BLANCHE: Samson! Go on, lift me. (*He comes behind her
and puts his hand on her waist and raises her lightly off
the ground.*) Well?

71

MITCH: You are light as a feather.

BLANCHE: Ha-ha! (*He lowers her but keeps his hands on her waist.* BLANCHE *speaks with an affectation of demureness.*) You may release me now. Not being his self. Gone all day.

MITCH: Huh?

BLANCHE (*gaily*): I said unhand me, sir. (*He fumbling embraces her. Her voice sounds gently reproving.*) Now, Mitch. Just because Stanley and Stella aren't at home is no reason why you shouldn't behave like a gentleman.

she could be scared that she'd betray herself

MITCH: Just give me a slap whenever I step out of bounds.

BLANCHE: That won't be necessary. You're a natural gentleman, one of the very few that are left in the world. I don't want you to think that I am severe and old maid school-teacherish or anything like that. It's just – well –

MITCH: Huh?

BLANCHE: I guess it it just that I have – old-fashioned ideals! (*She rolls her eyes, knowing he cannot see her face.* MITCH *goes to the front door. There is a considerable silence between them.* BLANCHE *sighs and* MITCH *coughs self-consciously.*)

she's pulled in a way she wants him but has got to appear a lady

MITCH (*finally*): Where's Stanley and Stella tonight?

BLANCHE: They have gone out. With Mr and Mrs Hubbel upstairs.

MITCH: Where did they go?

BLANCHE: I think they were planning to go to a midnight prevue at Loew's State.

MITCH: We should all go out together some night.

BLANCHE: No. That wouldn't be a good plan.

reminder that's us on her track. fear comes to surface

MITCH: Why not?

BLANCHE: You are an old friend of Stanley's?

MITCH: We was together in the Two-forty-first.

BLANCHE: I guess he talks to you frankly?

MITCH: Sure.

BLANCHE: Has he talked to you about me? ~worried~

MITCH: Oh – not very much.

BLANCHE: The way you say that, I suspect that he has.

MITCH: No, he hasn't said much.

BLANCHE: But what he *has* said. What would you say his attitude toward me was?

MITCH: Why do you want to ask that?

BLANCHE: Well –

MITCH: Don't you get along with him?

BLANCHE: What do you think?   *evidence that St. M have talked about her*

MITCH: I don't think he understands you.

BLANCHE: That is putting it mildly. If it weren't for Stella about to have a baby, I wouldn't be able to endure things here.

MITCH: He isn't – nice to you?

BLANCHE: He is insufferably rude. Goes out of his way to offend me.   *Trying to turn M. against St. Did same thing with S.*

MITCH: In what way, Blanche?

BLANCHE: Why, in every conceivable way.

MITCH: I'm surprised to hear that.

BLANCHE: Are you?

MITCH: Well, I – don't see how anybody could be rude to you.

BLANCHE: It's really a pretty frightful situation. You see, there's no privacy here. There's just these portières between the two rooms at night. He stalks through the rooms in his underwear at night. And I have to ask him to close the bathroom door. That sort of commonness isn't necessary. You probably wonder why I don't move out. Well, I'll tell you frankly. A teacher's salary is barely sufficient for her living-expenses. I didn't save a penny last year and so I had to come here for the summer. That's why I have to put up with my sister's   *very aware of his physical presence   Threat from S.*

husband. And he has to put up with me, apparently so much against his wishes . . . Surely he must have told you how much he hates me!

MITCH: I don't think he hates you.

BLANCHE: He hates me. Or why would he insult me? Of course there is such a thing as the hostility of – perhaps in some perverse kind of way he – No! To think of it makes me . . . (*She makes a gesture of revulsion. Then she finishes her drink. A pause follows.*)

MITCH: Blanche –

BLANCHE: Yes, honey?

MITCH: Can I ask you a question?

BLANCHE: Yes. What?

MITCH: How old are you?

    She makes a nervous gesture.

BLANCHE: Why do you want to know?

MITCH: I talked to my mother about you and she said, "How old is Blanche?" And I wasn't able to tell her. (*There is another pause.*)

BLANCHE: You talked to your mother about me?

MITCH: Yes.

BLANCHE: Why?

MITCH: I told my mother how nice you were, and I liked you.

BLANCHE: Were you sincere about that?

MITCH: You know I was.

BLANCHE: Why did your mother want to know my age?

BLANCHE: Mother is sick.

BLANCHE: I'm sorry to hear it. Badly?

MITCH: She won't live long. Maybe just a few months.

BLANCHE: Oh.

MITCH: She worries because I'm not settled.

74

M is very vulnerable

BLANCHE: Oh.

MITCH: She wants me to be settled down before she – (*His voice is hoarse and he clears his throat twice, shuffling nervously around with his hands in and out of his pockets.*)

BLANCHE: You love her very much, don't you?

MITCH: Yes.

BLANCHE: I think you have a great capacity for devotion. You will be lonely when she passes on, won't you? (MITCH *clears his throat and nods.*) I understand what that is.

MITCH: To be lonely?

BLANCHE: I loved someone, too, and the person I loved I lost.

MITCH: Dead? (*She crosses to the window and sits on the sill, looking out. She pours herself another drink.*) A man?

BLANCHE: He was a boy, just a boy, when I was a very young girl. When I was sixteen, I made the discovery – love. All at once and much, much too completely. It was like you suddenly turned a blinding light on something that had always been half in shadow, that's how it struck the world for me. But I was unlucky. Deluded. There was something different about the boy, a nervousness, a softness and tenderness which wasn't like a man's, although he wasn't the least bit effeminate looking – still – that thing was there . . . He came to me for help. I didn't know that. I didn't find out anything till after our marriage when we'd run away and come back and all I knew was I'd failed him in some mysterious way and wasn't able to give the help he needed but couldn't speak of! He was in the quicksands and clutching at me – but I wasn't holding him out, I was slipping in with him! I didn't know that. I didn't know anything except I loved

75

him unendurably but without being able to help him or help myself. Then I found out. In the worst of all possible ways. <u>By coming suddenly into a room that I thought was empty</u> – which wasn't empty, but had two people in it . . . *he was gay*

A locomotive is heard approaching outside. She claps her hands to her ears and crouches over. <u>The headlight of the locomotive glares into the room</u> as it thunders past. As the noise recedes she straightens slowly and continues speaking.

light comes in at crucial moment – the hurt

BLANCHE: Afterwards we pretended that nothing had been discovered. Yes, the three of us drove out to Moon Lake Casino, very drunk and laughing all the way.

Polka music sounds, in a <u>minor</u> key faint with distance.

BLANCHE: We danced the Varsouviana! Suddenly in the middle of the dance the boy I had married broke away from me and ran out of the casino. A few moments later – a shot!

The Polka stops abruptly. BLANCHE *rises stiffly. Then the Polka resumes in a <u>major</u> key.*

BLANCHE: I ran out – all did! – all ran and gathered about the terrible thing at the edge of the lake! I couldn't get near for the crowding. Then somebody caught my arm. "Don't go any closer! Come back! You don't want to see!" See? See what! Then I heard voices say – Allan! Allan! The Grey boy! He'd stuck the revolver into his mouth, and fired – so that the back of his head had been – blown away!

She sways and covers her face.

76

BLANCHE: It was because – on the dance-floor – unable to stop myself – I'd suddenly said – "I know! I know! You disgust me . . ." And then the searchlight which had been turned on the world was turned off again and never for one moment since has there been any light that's stronger than this – kitchen – candle . . .

[handwritten margin note: she knew the secret.]

[handwritten margin note: different light turned on when she found out he was gay]

    MITCH *gets up awkwardly and moves towards her a little. The Polka music increases.* MITCH *stands beside her.*

MITCH (*drawing her slowly into his arms*): You need somebody. And I need somebody, too. Could it be – you and me, Blanche?

    She stares at him vacantly for a moment. Then with a soft cry huddles in his embrace. She makes a sobbing effort to speak but the words won't come. He kisses her forehead and her eyes and finally her lips. The Polka tune fades out. Her breath is drawn and released in long, grateful sobs.

BLANCHE: Sometimes – there's God – so quickly!

[handwritten notes: Polka music reminds her of him.]

[handwritten notes: Two pages have been confession.]

[handwritten notes: After confession is forgiveness.]

[handwritten notes: She feels forgiven by M]

[handwritten notes: feel sorry for B here]

SCENE VII

It is late afternoon in mid-September. The portières are open and a table is set for a birthday supper, with cake and flowers. STELLA *is completing the decorations as* STANLEY *comes in.*

STANLEY: What's all this stuff for?

STELLA: Honey, it's Blanche's birthday.

STANLEY: She here?

STELLA: In the bathroom.

STANLEY (*mimicking*): "Washing out some things"?

STELLA: I reckon so.

STANLEY: How long she been in there?

STELLA: All afternoon.

STANLEY (*mimicking*): "Soaking in a hot tub"?

STELLA: Yes.

STANLEY: Temperature 100 on the nose, and she soaks herself in a hot tub.

STELLA: She says it cools her off for the evening.

STANLEY: And you run out an' get her cokes, I suppose? And serve 'em to Her Majesty in the tub? (STELLA *shrugs.*) Set down here a minute.

STELLA: Stanley, I've got things to do.

STANLEY: Set down! I've got th' dope on your big sister, Stella.

STELLA: Stanley, stop picking on Blanche.

STANLEY: That girl calls *me* common!

STELLA: Lately you have been doing all you can think of to rub her the wrong way, Stanley, and Blanche is sensitive and you've got to realize that Blanche and I grew up under very different circumstances than you did.

STANLEY: So I been told. And told and told and told! You

78

know she's been feeding us a pack of lies here?

STELLA: No, I don't, and –

STANLEY: Well, she has, however. But now that cat's out of the bag! I found out some things!

STELLA: What – things?

STANLEY: Things I already suspected. But now I got proof from the most reliable sources – which I have checked on!

Doesn't think of her feelings. Enjoys telling it. Doesn't blurt it all out at once.

BLANCHE *is singing in the bathroom a saccharine popular ballad which is used contrapunctually with* STANLEY'S *speech.*

Can B hear St? Why does she sing so loud?

STELLA (*to* STANLEY): Lower your voice!

STANLEY: Some canary-bird, huh!

STELLA: Now please tell me quietly what you think you've found out about my sister.

STANLEY: Lie Number One: All this squeamishness she puts on! You should just know the line she's been feeding to Mitch. He thought she had never been more than kissed by a fellow! But Sister Blanche is no lily! Ha-ha! Some lily she is!

STELLA: What have you heard and who from?

STANLEY: Our supply-man down at the plant had been going through Laurel for years and he knows all about her and everybody else in the town of Laurel knows all about her. She is as famous in Laurel as if she was the President of the United States, only she is not respected by any party! This supply-man stops at a hotel called the Flamingo.

BLANCHE (*singing blithely*):

"Say, it's only a paper moon, Sailing over a cardboard sea –

But it wouldn't be make-believe If you believed in me!"

STELLA: What about the – Flamingo?

STANLEY: She stayed there, too.

STELLA: My sister lived at Belle Reve.

STANLEY: This is after the home-place had slipped through her lily-white fingers! She moved to the Flamingo! A second-class hotel which has the advantage of not interfering in the private social life of the personalities there! The Flamingo is used to all kinds of goings-on. But even the management of the Flamingo was impressed by Dame Blanche! In fact they were so impressed by Dame Blanche that they requested her to turn in her room-key – for permanent! This happened a couple of weeks before she showed here.

BLANCHE (*singing*):

"It's a Barnum and Bailey world, Just as phony as it can be –

But it wouldn't be make-believe If you believed in me!"

STELLA: What – contemptible – lies!

STANLEY: Sure, I can see how you would be upset by this. She pulled the wool over your eyes as much as Mitch's!

STELLA: It's pure invention! There's not a word of truth in it and if I were a man and this creature had dared to invent such things in my presence –

BLANCHE (*singing*):

"Without your love,

It's a honky-tonk parade!

Without your love,

It's a melody played in a penny arcade . . ."

STANLEY: Honey, I told you I thoroughly checked on these stories! Now wait till I finished. The trouble with Dame Blanche was that she couldn't put on her act any more in Laurel! They got wised up after two or three dates with her and then they quit, and she goes on to another, the same old lines, same old act, same old hooey! But the town was too small for this to go on forever! And as time went by she became a town character. <u>Regarded as not just different but downright loco – nuts.</u> *related to end*

STELLA *draws back.*

STANLEY: And for the last year or two she has been washed up like poison. That's why she's here this summer, visiting royalty, putting on all this act – because she's practically told by the mayor to get out of town! Yes, did you know there was an army camp near Laurel and your sister's was one of the places called "Out-of-Bounds"?

BLANCHE:
"It's only a paper moon, just as phoney as it can be –
But it wouldn't be make-believe If you believed in me!"

STANLEY: Well, so much for her being such a refined and particular type of girl. Which brings us to Lie Number Two.

STELLA: I don't want to hear any more!

STANLEY: She's not going back to teach school! In fact I am willing to bet you that she never had no idea of returning to Laurel! She didn't resign temporarily from the high school because of her nerves! No, siree, Bob! She didn't. They kicked her out of that high school before the spring term ended – and I hate to tell you the reason that step was taken! A seventeen-year-old boy – she'd gotten mixed up with! *B-hood*

BLANCHE:
"It's a Barnum and Bailey world, Just as phony as it can be –"

In the bathroom the water goes on loud; little breathless

had no other choice but to come to 81
t. she was trapped

cries and peals of laughter are heard as if a child were frolicking in the tub.

STELLA: This is making me – sick!

STANLEY: The boy's dad learned about it and got in touch with the high school superintendent. Boy, oh, boy, I'd like to have been in that office when Dame Blanche was called on the carpet! I'd like to have seen her trying to squirm out of that one! But they had her on the hook good and proper that time and she knew that the jig was all up! They told her she better move on to some fresh territory. Yep, it was practickly a town ordinance passed against her!

The bathroom door is open and BLANCHE *thrusts her head out holding a towel about her hair.*

BLANCHE: Stella!

STELLA (*faintly*): Yes, Blanche?

BLANCHE: Give me another bath-towel to dry my hair with. I've just washed it.

STELLA: Yes, Blanche.

She crosses in a dazed way from the kitchen to the bathroom door with a towel.

BLANCHE: What's the matter, honey?

STELLA: Matter? Why?

BLANCHE: You have such a strange expression on your face!

STELLA: Oh – (*She tries to laugh.*) I guess I'm a little tired!

BLANCHE: Why don't you bathe, too, soon as I get out?

STANLEY (*calling from the kitchen*): How soon is that going to be?

BLANCHE: Not so terribly long! Possess your soul in patience!

STANLEY: It's not my soul I'm worried about!

BLANCHE *slams the door.* STANLEY *laughs harshly.* STELLA *comes slowly back into the kitchen.*

STANLEY: Well, what do you think of it?

STELLA: I don't believe all of those stories and I think your supply-man was mean and rotten to tell them. It's possible that some of the things he said are partly true. There are things about my sister I don't approve of – things that caused sorrow at home. She was always – flighty! She realises

STANLEY: Flighty is some word for it!

STELLA: But when she was young, very young, she had an experience that – killed her illusions!

STANLEY: What experience was that?

STELLA: I mean her marriage, when she was – almost a child! She married a boy who wrote poetry . . . He was extremely good-looking. I think Blanche didn't just love him but worshipped the ground he walked on! Adored him and thought him almost too fine to be human! But then she found out –

STANLEY: What?

STELLA: This beautiful and talented young man was a degenerate. Didn't your supply-man give you that information?

STANLEY: All we discussed was recent history. That must have been a pretty long time ago. feels a bit bad now.

STELLA: Yes, it was – a pretty long time ago . . .

STANLEY *comes up and takes her by the shoulders rather gently. She gently withdraws from him. Automatically she starts sticking little pink candles in the birthday cake.*

STANLEY: How many candles are you putting in that cake?

STELLA: I'll stop at twenty-five.

STANLEY: Is company expected?

STELLA: We asked Mitch to come over for cake and ice-cream.

> STANLEY *looks a little uncomfortable. He lights a cigarette from the one he has just finished.*

STANLEY: I wouldn't be expecting Mitch over tonight.

> STELLA *pauses in her occupation with candles and looks slowly around at* STANLEY.

STELLA: *Why*?

STANLEY: Mitch is a buddy of mine. We were in the same outfit together – Two-forty-first Engineers. We work in the same plant and now on the same bowling team. You think I could face him if –

STELLA: Stanley Kowalski, did you – did you repeat what that . . . ?

STANLEY: You're goddam right I told him! I'd have that on my conscience the rest of my life if I knew all that stuff and let my best friend get caught!

STELLA: Mitch is through with her?

STANLEY: Wouldn't you be if . . . ?

STELLA: I said, *Is Mitch through with her?*

> BLANCHE'S *voice is lifted again, serenely as a bell. She sings "But it wouldn't be make-believe If you believed in me."*

STANLEY: No, I don't think he's necessarily through with her – just wised up!

STELLA: Stanley, she thought Mitch was – going to – going to marry her. I was hoping so, too.

STANLEY: Well, he's not going to marry her. Maybe he *was*,

but he's not going to jump in a tank with a school of sharks – now!

He rises.

STANLEY: Blanche! Oh, Blanche! Can I please get in my bathroom?

There is a pause.

BLANCHE: Yes, indeed, sir! Can you wait one second while I dry?

STANLEY: Having waited one hour I guess one second ought to pass in a hurry.

STELLA: And she hasn't got her job? Well, what will she do!

STANLEY: She's not stayin' here after Tuesday. You know that. don't you? Just to make sure I bought her ticket myself. A bus-ticket!

STELLA: In the first place, Blanche wouldn't go on a bus.

STANLEY: She'll go on a bus and like it.

STELLA: No, she won't, no, she won't, Stanley!

STANLEY: *She'll go!* Period. P.S. She'll go *Tuesday*!

STELLA (*slowly*): What'll – she – do? What on earth will she – *do*!

STANLEY: Her future is mapped out for her.

STELLA: What do you mean?

BLANCHE *sings.*

STANLEY: Hey, canary bird! Toots! Get *OUT* of the *BATHROOM*! Must I speak more plainly?

The bathroom door flies open and BLANCHE *emerges with a gay peal of laughter, but as* STANLEY *crosses past her, a frightened look appears in her face, almost a look of panic. He doesn't look at her but slams the bathroom door shut as he goes in.*

BLANCHE (*snatching up a hair-brush*): Oh, I feel so good after my long, hot bath, I feel so good and cool and – rested!

STELLA (*sadly and doubtfully from the kitchen*): Do you, Blanche?

BLANCHE (*brushing her hair vigorougly*): Yes, I do, so refreshed. (*She tinkles her highball glass.*) A hot bath and a long, cold drink always gives me a brand new outlook on life!

 mnic, Her 2 props= bath r drink

She looks through the portières at STELLA, *standing between them, and slowly stops brushing.*

BLANCHE: Something has happened! – What is it?

STELLA (*turning quickly away*): Why, nothing has happened, Blanche.

BLANCHE: You're lying! Something has!

She stares fearfully at STELLA, *who pretends to be busy at the table. The distant piano goes into a hectic breakdown.*

B is trapped now.
St has told M ☉ bought her a bus ticket.
Everything changes

SCENE VIII

Three-quarters of an hour later.

The view through the big windows is fading gradually into a still-golden dusk. A torch of sunlight blazes on the side of a big water-tank or oil-drum across the empty lot toward the business district which is now pierced by pinpoints of lighted windows or windows reflecting the sunset, symbolizes fading hope

The three people are completing a dismal birthday supper. STANLEY looks sullen. STELLA is embarrassed and sad. BLANCHE has a tight, artificial smile on her drawn face. There is a fourth place at the table which is left vacant. happy dreaming at the those

BLANCHE (*suddenly*): Stanley, tell us a joke, tell us a funny story to make us all laugh. I don't know what's the matter, we're all so solemn. Is it because I've beem stood up by my beau? old Belle Reve language

STANLEY *laughs feebly.* - feels ab + guilty

BLANCHE: It's the first time in my entire experience with men, and I've had a good deal of all sorts, that I've actually been stood up by anybody! Ha-ha! I don't know how to take it . . . Tell us a funny little story, Stanley! Something to help us out.

STANLEY: I didn't think you liked my stories, Blanche.

BLANCHE: I like them when they're amusing but not indecent. always reminding him that he's common

STANLEY: I don't know any refined enough for your taste.

BLANCHE: Then let me tell one.

STELLA: Yes, you tell one, Blanche. You used to know lots

of good stories.

The music fades.

BLANCHE: Let me see, now . . . I must run through my repertoire! Oh, yes – I love parrot stories! Do you all like parrot stories? Well, this one's about an old maid and the parrot. This old maid, she had a parrot that cursed a blue streak and knew more vulgar expressions than Mr Kowalski!

STANLEY: Huh.

BLANCHE: And the only way to hush the parrot was to put the cover back on its cage so it would think it was night and go back to sleep. Well, one morning the old maid had just uncovered the parrot for the day – when who should she see coming up the front walk but the preacher! Well, she rushed back to the parrot and slipped the cover back on the cage and then she let in the preacher. And the parrot was perfectly still, just as quiet as a mouse, but just as she was asking the preacher how much sugar he wanted in his coffee – the parrot broke the silence with a loud – (*she whistles*) – and said – "God *damn*, but that was a short day!"

She throws back her head and laughs, STELLA *also makes an ineffectual effort to seem amused.* STANLEY *pays no attention to the story but reaches way over the table to spear his fork into the remaining chop which he eats with his fingers.*

BLANCHE: Apparently Mr Kowalski was not amused.

STELLA: Mr Kowalski is too busy making a pig of himself to think of anything else!

STANLEY: That's right, baby.

STELLA: Your face and your fingers are disgustingly greasy.

Go and wash up and then help me clear the table.

He hurls a plate to the floor.

STANLEY: That's how I'll clear the table! (*He seizes her arm.*) Don't ever talk that way to me! "Pig – Polack – disgusting – vulgar – greasy!" – them kind of words have been on your tongue and your sister's too much around here! What do you two think you are? A pair of queens? Remember what Huey Long said – "Every Man is a King!" And I am the king around here, so don't forget it! (*He hurls a cup and saucer to the floor.*) My place is cleared! You want me to clear your plates?

STELLA *begins to cry weakly.* STANLEY *stalks out on the porch and lights a cigarette. The Negro entertainers around the corner are heard.*

BLANCHE: What happened while I was bathing? What did he tell you, Stella?

STELLA: Nothing, nothing, nothing!

BLANCHE: I think he told you something about Mitch and me! You know why Mitch didn't come but you won't tell me!

STELLA *shakes her head helplessly.*

BLANCHE: I'm going to call him!

STELLA: I wouldn't call him, Blanche.

BLANCHE: I am. I'm going to call him on the phone.

STELLA (*miserably*): I wish you wouldn't.

BLANCHE: I intend to be given some explanation from someone!

She rushes to the phone in the bathroom. STELLA *goes out on the porch and stares reproachfully at her husband.*

He grunts and turns away from her.

[handwritten: animal]

STELLA: I hope you're pleased with your doings. I never had so much trouble swallowing food in my life, looking at the girl's face and the empty chair.

[handwritten: sees vulnerability in B]

She cries quietly.

[handwritten: B desperately looking for a lifeline, she knows something]

BLANCHE (*at the phone*): Hello. Mr Mitchell, please . . . Oh . . . I would like to leave a number if I may. Magnolia 9047. And say it's important to call . . . Yes, very important . . . Thank you.

She remains by the phone with a lost, frightened look. STANLEY *turns slowly back towards his wife and takes her clumsily in his arms.*

[handwritten: We find out how st feels about B invading privacy, strongest in close quarters]

STANLEY: Stell, it's gonna be all right after she goes and after you've had the baby. It's gonna be all right again between you and me the way it was. You remember that way it was? Them nights we had together? God, honey, it's gonna be sweet when we can make noise in the night the way that we used to and get the coloured lights going with nobody's sister behind the curtains to hear us!

[handwritten: don't know how s reacts]

Their upstairs neighbours are heard in bellowing laughter at something. STANLEY *chuckles.*

[handwritten: lightens things]

[handwritten: As side now she has been removed]

STELLA: Come on back in. (*She returns to the kitchen and starts lighting the candles on the white cake.*) Blanche?

BLANCHE: Yes. (*She returns from the bedroom to the table in the kitchen.*) Oh, those pretty, pretty little candles! Oh, don't burn them, Stella.

STELLA: I certainly will.

STANLEY *comes back in.*

BLANCHE: You ought to save them for baby's birthdays.

NOTES — love? story of her life + marriage.

Oh, I hope candles are going to glow in his life and I hope that his eyes are going to be like candles, like two blue candles lighted in a white cake!

STANLEY (*sitting down*): What poetry!

BLANCHE: His Auntie knows candles aren't safe, that candles burn out in little boys' and girls' eyes, or wind blows them out and after that happens, electric light bulbs go on and you see too plainly . . . (*She pauses reflectively for a moment.*) I shouldn't have called him.

STELLA: There's lots of things could have happened.

BLANCHE: There's no excuse for it, Stella. I don't have to put up with insults. I won't be taken for granted.

STANLEY: Goddamn, it's hot in here with the steam from the bathroom. tense atmosphere

BLANCHE: I've said I was sorry three times. (*The piano fades out.*) I take hot baths for my nerves. Hydro-therapy, they call it. You healthy Polack, without a nerve in your body, of course you don't know what anxiety feels like!

STANLEY: I am not a Polack. People from Poland are Poles, not Polacks. But what I am is a one hundred per cent. American, born and raised in the greatest country on earth and proud as hell of it, so don't ever call me a Polack. B + St can't help insulting each other

The phone rings. BLANCHE *rises expectantly.*

BLANCHE: Oh, that's for me, I'm sure.

STANLEY: *I'm* not sure. Keep your seat. (*He crosses leisurely to the phone.*) H'lo. Aw, yeh, hello, Mac.

He leans against wall, staring insultingly in at BLANCHE. *She sinks back in her chair with a frightened look.* STELLA *leans over and touches her shoulder.*

BLANCHE: Oh, keep your hands off me, Stella. What is the

91

matter with you? Why do you look at me with that pitying look?

STANLEY: (*bawling*): QUIET IN THERE! – We've got a noisy woman on the place. – Go on, Mac. At Riley's? No, I don't wanta bowl at Riley's. I had a little trouble with Riley last week. I'm the team-captain, ain't I? All right, then, we're not gonna bowl at Riley's, we're gonna bowl at the West Side or the Gala! All right, Mac. See you!

He hangs up and returns to the table. BLANCHE *fiercly controls herself, drinking quietly from her tumbler of water. He doesn't look at her but reaches in a pocket. Then he speaks slowly and with false amiability.*

STANLEY: Sister Blanche, I've got a little birthday remembrance for you.

BLANCHE: Oh, have you, Stanley? I wasn't expecting any, I – I don't know why Stella wants to observe my birthday! I'd much rather forget it – when you – reach twenty-seven! Well – age is a subject that you'd prefer to – ignore!

STANLEY: Twenty-seven?

BLANCHE (*quickly*): What is it? Is it for *me*?

He is holding a little envelope towards her.

STANLEY: Yes, I hope you like it!

BLANCHE: Why, why – Why, it's a –

STANLEY: Ticket! Back to Laurel! On the Greyhound! Tuesday!

The Varsouviana music steals in softly and continues playing. STELLA *rises abruptly and turns her back.* BLANCHE *tries to smile. Then she tries to laugh. Then she gives both up and springs from the table and runs into the next room. She clutches her throat and then runs into the bathroom. Coughing, gagging sounds are heard.*

STANLEY: Well!

STELLA: You didn't need to do that.

STANLEY: Don't forget all that I took off her.

STELLA: You needn't have been so cruel to someone alone as she is.

STANLEY: Delicate piece she is.

STELLA: She is. She was. You don't know Blanche as a girl. Nobody, nobody, was tender and trusting as she was. But people like you abused her, and forced her to change.

He crosses into the bedroom, ripping off his shirt, and changes into a brilliant silk bowling shirt. She follows him.

STELLA: Do you think you're going bowling now?

STANLEY: Sure.

STELLA: You're not going bowling. (*She catches hold of his shirt.*) Why did you do this to her?

STANLEY: I done nothing to no one. Let go of my shirt. You've torn it.

STELLA: I want to know why first. Tell me why.

STANLEY: When we first met, me and you, you thought I was common. How right you was, baby. I was common as dirt. You showed me the snapshot of the place with columns. I pulled you down off them columns and how you loved it, having them coloured lights going! And wasn't we happy together, wasn't it all okay till she showed here?

STELLA *makes a slight movement. Her look goes*

93

suddenly inward as if some interior voice had called her name. She begins a slow, shuffling progress from the bedroom to the kitchen, leaning and resting on the back of the chair and then on the edge of the table with a blind look and listening expression. STANLEY, *finishing with his shirt, is unaware of her reaction.*

STANLEY: And wasn't we happy together! Wasn't it all okay? Till she showed here. Hoity-toity, describing me as an ape. (*He suddenly notices the change in* STELLA.) Hey, what is it, Stel? (*He crosses to her.*)

STELLA (*quietly*): Take me to the hospital.

He is with her now, supporting her with his arm, murmuring indistinguishably as they go outside. The "Varsouviana" is heard, its music rising with sinister rapidity as the bathroom door opens slightly. BLANCHE *comes out twisting a washcloth. She begins to whisper the words as the light fades slowly.*

BLANCHE: *El pan de mais, el pan de mais,*
   El pan de mais, sin sal.
   El pan de mais, el pan de mais,
   El pan de mais sin sal . . .

Now stella has gone, it is just B + st. There is no te there to keep the peace

SCENE IX

B. faces up to the truth in this scene

A *while later that evening.* BLANCHE *is seated in a tense hunched position in a bedroom chair that she has re-covered with diagonal green and white stripes. She has on her scarlet satin robe. On the table beside the chair is a bottle of liquor and a glass. The rapid, feverish polka tune, the "Varsouviana", is heard. The music is in her mind; she is drinking to escape it and the sense of disaster closing in on her, and she seems to whisper the words of the song. An electric fan is turning back and forth across her.* *very aware of it.*

MITCH *comes around the corner in work clothes: blue denim shirt and pants. He is unshaven. He climbs the steps to the door and rings,* BLANCHE *is startled.*

Not trying to make an impression any more - Not showing any respect for her any more.

BLANCHE: Who is it, please?
MITCH (*hoarsely*): Me. Mitch.

Why HAS HE COME? He feels a bit foolish. Wants an explanation

The polka tune stops.

BLANCHE: Mitch! – Just a minute.

She rushes about frantically, hiding the bottle in a closet, crouching at the mirror and dabbing her face with cologne and powder. She is so excited that her breath is audible as she dashes about. At last she rushes to the door in the kitchen and lets him in. *Suddenly gets herself into a state*

BLANCHE: Mitch! – Y'now, I really shouldn't let you in after the treatment I have received from you this evening! So utterly uncavalier! But hello, beautiful! *Puts on her usual act*

many lies

She offers him her lips. He ignores it and pushes past

+ she had been honest in the first place she may have been accepted.

95

her into the flat. She looks fearfully after him as he stalks into the bedroom.

BLANCHE: My, my, what a cold shoulder! And a face like a thundercloud! And such uncouth apparel! Why, you haven't even shaven! The unforgivable insult to a lady! But I forgive you. I forgive you because it's such a relief to see you. You've stopped that polka tune that I had caught in my head. Have you ever had anything caught in your head? Some words, a piece of music? That goes relentlessly on and on in your head? No, of course you haven't, you dumb angel-puss, you'd never get anything awful caught in your head!

He stares at her while she follows him while she talks. It is obvious that he has had a few drinks on the way over.

MITCH: Do we have to have the fan on?

BLANCHE: No!

MITCH: I don't like fans.

BLANCHE: Then let's turn it off, honey. I'm not partial to them!

She presses the switch and the fan nods slowly off. She clears her throat uneasily as MITCH *plumps himself down on the bed in the bedroom and lights a cigarette.*

BLANCHE: I don't know what there is to drink. I – haven't investigated?

MITCH: I don't want Stan's liquor.

BLANCHE: It isn't Stan's. Everything here isn't Stan's. Some things on the premises are actually mine! How is your mother? Isn't you mother well?

MITCH: Why?

BLANCHE: Something'd the matter tonight, but never mind. I won't cross-examine the witness. I'll just – (*She touches*

96

her forehead vaguely. The polka tune starts up again.) – pretend I don't notice anything different about you! That – music again . . .

MITCH: What music?

BLANCHE: The "Varsouvania"? The polka tune they were playing when Allan – Wait!

A distant revolver shot is heard. BLANCHE *seems relieved.*

BLANCHE: There now, the shot! It always stops after that.

The polka tune music dies out again.

BLANCHE: Yes, now it's stopped.

MITCH: Are you boxed out of your mind?

BLANCHE: I'll go and see what I can find in the way of – (*She crosses into the closet, pretending to search for a bottle.*) Oh, by the way, excuse me for not being dressed. But I'd practically given you up! Had you forgotten you invitation to supper?

MITCH: I wasn't going to see you any more.

BLANCHE: Wait a minute. I can't hear what you're saying and you talk so little that when you do say something, I don't want to miss a single syllable of it . . . What am I looking around here for? Oh, yes – liquor! We've had so much excitement around here this evening that I *am* boxed out of my mind! (*She pretends suddenly to find the bottle.* He draws his foot up on the bed and stares at her contemptuously.*) Here's something. Southern Comfort! What is that, I wonder?

MITCH: If you don't know, it must belong to Stan.

BLANCHE: Take your foot off the bed. It has a light cover on it. Of course you boys don't notice things like that. I've done so much with this place since I've been here.

MITCH: <u>I bet you have.</u> *sarcasm*

BLANCHE: You saw it before I came. Well, look at it now! <u>This room us almost – dainty!</u> <u>I want to keep it that way.</u> I wonder if this stuff ought to be mixed with something? Ummm, it's sweet, so sweet! It's terribly, terribly sweet! Why, it's a *liqueur*, I believe! Yes, that's what it *is*, a liqueur! (MITCH *grunts*.) I'm afraid you won't like it, but try it, and maybe you will.

MITCH: I told you already I don't want none of his liquor and I mean it. You ought to lay off his liquor. He says you been lapping it up all summer like a wild-cat!

BLANCHE: What a <u>fantastic</u> statement! <u>Fantastic</u> of him saying it, fantastic of you to repeat it! I won't descend to the level of such) cheap accusations to answer them, even! *extreme reaction –*

MITCH: Huh. *she beging it*

BLANCHE: <u>What's in your mind? I see something in your eyes!</u>

MITCH (*getting up*): It's dark in here. *feels safer in the dark.*

BLANCHE: <u>I like it dark. The dark is comforting to me.</u>

MITCH: I don't think I ever seen you in the light. (BLANCHE *laughs breathlessly*.) That's a fact!

BLANCHE: Is it?

MITCH: I've never seen you in the afternoon.

BLANCHE: Whose fault is that?

MITCH: You never go out in the afternoon.

BLANCHE: Why, Mitch, you're at the plant in the afternoon!

MITCH: Not Sunday afternoon. I've asked you to go out with me sometimes on Sundays but you always make an excuse. You never want to go out till six and then it's always some place that's not lighted much.

BLANCHE: There is some obscure meaning in this but I fail to catch it.

MITCH: What it means is I've never had a real look at you, Blanche.

BLANCHE: What are you leading up to?

MITCH: Let's turn the light on here.

BLANCHE (*fearfully*): Light? Which light? What for?

MITCH: This one with the paper thing on it. (*He tears the paper lantern off the light bulb. She utters a frightened gasp.*)

BLANCHE: What did you do that for?

MITCH: So I can take a look at you good and plain!

BLANCHE: Of course you don't really mean to be insulting!

MITCH: No, just realistic.

BLANCHE: I don't want realism.

MITCH: Naw, I guess not.

BLANCHE: I'll tell you what I want. Magic! (MITCH *laughs.*) Yes, yes, magic! I try to give that to people. I misrepresent things to them. I don't tell the truth, I tell what *ought* to be the truth. And if that is sinful, then let me be damned for it! – *Don't turn the light on!*

MITCH *crosses to the switch. He turns the light on and stares at her. She cries out and covers her face. He turns the light off again.*

MITCH (*slowly and bitterly*): I don't mind you being older than what I thought. But the rest of it – God! That pitch about your ideals being so old-fashioned and all the malarky that you've dished out all summer. Oh, I knew you weren't sixteen any more. But I was a fool enough to believe you was straight.

BLANCHE: Who told you I wasn't – "straight"? My loving brother-in-law. And you believed him.

MITCH: I called him a liar at first. And then I checked on the story. First I asked our supply-man who travels through

99

Laurel. And then I talked directly over long-distance to this merchant.

BLANCHE: Who is the merchant?

MITCH: Kiefaber.

BLANCHE: The merchant Kiefaber of Laurel! I know the man. He whistled at me. I put him in his place. So now for revenge he makes up stories about me.

MITCH: Three people, Kiefaber, Stanley and Shaw, swore to them!

BLANCHE: Rub-a-dub-dub, three men in a tub! And such a filthy tub!

MITCH: Didn't you stay at a hotel called The Flamingo?

BLANCHE: Flamingo? No! Tarantula was the name of it! I stayed at a hotel called The Tarantula Arms!

MITCH (*stupidly*): Tarantula?

BLANCHE: Yes, a big spider! That's where I brought my victims. (*She pours herself another drink.*) Yes, I had many intimacies with strangers. After the death of Allan – the intimacies with strangers was all I seemed able to fill my empty head with . . . I think it was panic, just panic, that drove me from one to another, hunting for some protection – here and there, in the most – unlikely places – even, at last, in a seventeen-year-old boy but – somebody wrote the superintendent about it – "This woman is morally unfit for her position!"

She throws back her head with convulsive, sobbing laughter. Then she repeats the statement, gasps, and drinks.

BLANCHE: True? Yes, I suppose – unfit somehow – anyway . . . So I came here. There was nowhere else I could go. I was played out. You know what played out is? My youth was suddenly gone up the water-spout, and

– I met you. You said you needed somebody. Well, I needed somebody, too. I thanked God for you, because you seemed to be gentle – a cleft in the rock of the world that I could hide in! The poor man's Paradise – is a little peace . . . But I guess I was asking, hoping – too much! Kiefaber, Stanley and Shaw have tied an old tin can to the tail of the kite.

There is a pause. MITCH *stares at her dumbly.*

MITCH: You lied to me, Blanche.

BLANCHE: Don't say I lied to you.

MITCH: Lies, lies, inside and out, all lies.

BLANCHE: Never inside, I didn't lie in my heart . . .

A Vendor comes around the corner. She is a blind MEXICAN WOMAN *in a dark shawl, carrying bunches of gaudy tin flowers that lower class Mexicans display at funerals and other festive occasions. She is calling barely audibly. Her figure is only faintly visible outside the building.*

MEXICAN WOMAN: *Flores. Flores. Flores para los muertos. Flores. Flores.*

BLANCHE: What? Oh! Somebody outside . . . I – I lived in a house where dying old women remembered their dead men . . .

MEXICAN WOMAN: *Flores. Flores para los muertos* . . .

The polka tune fades in.

BLANCHE (*as if to herself*): Crumble and fade and – regrets – recriminations . . . "If you'd done this, it wouldn't've cost me that!"

MEXICAN WOMAN: *Corones pasra los muertos. Corones* . . .

BLANCHE: Legacies! Huh . . . And other things such as

blood-stained pillow-slips – "Her linen needs changing" – "Yes Mother. But couldn't we get a coloured girl to do it?" No, we couldn't of course. Everything gone but the . . .

MEXICAN WOMAN: *Flores.*

BLANCHE: <u>Death</u> – I used to sit here and she used to sit over there and death was as close as you are . . . We didn't dare even admit we had ever heard of it!

MEXICAN WOMAN: *Flores para los muertos, flores – flores . . .*

BLANCHE: The opposite is desire. So do you wonder? How could you possibly wonder! Not far from Belle Reve, before we had lost Belle Reve, was a camp where they trained young soldiers. On Saturday nights they would go in town to get drunk . . .

MEXICAN WOMAN (*softly*): *Corones . . .*

BLANCHE: – and on the way back they would stagger on to my lawn and call – "Blanche! Blanche!" – the deaf old lady remaining suspected nothing. But sometimes I slipped outside to answer their calls . . . Later the paddy-wagon would gather them up like daisies . . . the long way home . . .

The MEXICAN WOMAN *turns slowly and drifts back off with her soft mournful cries.* BLANCHE *goes to the dresser and leans forward on it. After a moment,* MITCH *rises and follows her purposefully. The polka music fades away. He places his hands on her waist and tries to turn her about.*

BLANCHE: What do you want?

MITCH (*fumbling to embrace her*): What I been missing all summer.

BLANCHE: Then marry me, Mitch!

102

MITCH: I don't think I want to marry you any more.

BLANCHE: No?

MITCH (*dropping his hands from her waist*): You're not ~~show~~ clean enough to bring in the house with my mother. *he hasn't*

BLANCHE: Go away, then. (*He stares at her.*) Get out of *under* here quick before I start screaming fire! (*Her throat is* *stood* *tightening with hysteria.*) Get out of here quick before I start screaming fire. *She has totally revealed herself & he has insulted her*

> He still remains staring. She suddenly rushes to the big
> window with its pale blue square of the soft summer light
> and cries wildly.

BLANCHE: Fire! Fire! Fire!

> With a startled gasp, MITCH *turns and goes out of the*
> *outer door, clatters awkwardly down the steps and around*
> *the corner of the building.* BLANCHE *staggers back from*
> *the window and falls to her knees. The distant piano is*
> *slow and blue.*

All these deaths drove her to desire so many people An explanation for the way that she behaves -

SCENE X

It is a few hours later that night. BLANCHE *has been drinking fairly steadily since* MITCH *left. She has dragged her wardrobe trunk into the centre of the bedroom. It hangs open with flowery dresses thrown across it. As the drinking and packing went on, a mood of hysterical exhilaration came into her and she has decked herself out in a somewhat soiled and crumpled white satin evening gown and a pair of scuffed silver slippers with brilliants set in their heels. Now she is replacing the rhinestone tiara on her head before the mirror of the dressing-table and murmuring excitedly as if to a group of spectral admirers.*

BLANCHE: How about taking a swim, a moonlight swim at the old rock-quarry? If anyone's sober enought to drive a car! Ha-Ha! Best way in the world to stop your head buzzing! Only you've got to be careful to dive where the deep pool is – if you hit a rock you don't come up till tomorrow . . .

Tremblingly she lifts the hand mirror for a closer inspection. She catches her breath and slams the mirror face down with such violence that the glass cracks. She moans a little and attempts to rise. STANLEY *appears around the corner of the building. He still has on the vivid green silk bowling shirt. As he rounds the corner the honky-tonk music is heard. It continues softly throughout the scene. He enters the kitchen, slamming the door. As he peers in at* BLANCHE, *he gives a low whistle. He has had a few drinks on the way and has brought some quart beer bottles home with him.*

BLANCHE: How is my sister?

104

STANLEY: She is doing okay.

BLANCHE: And how is the baby?

STANLEY (*grinning amiably*): The baby won't come before morning so they told me to go home and get a little shut-eye.

BLANCHE: Does that mean we are to be alone in here? *can't help herself*

STANLEY: Yep. Just me and you, Blanche. Unless you got somebody hid under the bed. What've you got on those fine feathers for? *Being nice.*

BLANCHE: Oh, that's right. You left before my wire came.

STANLEY: You got a wire? *Friendly, brotherly tease*

BLANCHE: I received a telegram from an old admirer of mine.

STANLEY: Anything good?

BLANCHE: I think so. An invitation. *She uses her language to set herself above him?*

STANLEY: What to? A fireman's ball?

BLANCHE (*throwing back her head*): A cruise of the Caribbean on a yacht!

STANLEY: Well, well. What do you know?

BLANCHE: I have never been so surprised in my life.

STANLEY: I guess not.

BLANCHE: It came like a bolt from the blue!

STANLEY: Who did you say it was from?

BLANCHE: An old beau of mine.

STANLEY: The one that ive you the white fox-pieces?

BLANCHE: Mr. Shep Huntleigh. I wore his ATO pin my last year at college. I hadn't seen him again until last Christmas. I ran in to him on Biscayne Boulevard. Then – just now – this wire – inviting me on a cruise of the Caribbean! The problem is clothes. I tore into my trunk to see what I have that's suitable for the tropics!

STANLEY: And come up with that – gorgeous – diamond – tiara? *laughing at her. She must look grotesque.*

BLANCHE: This old relic! Ha-ha! It's only rhinestones.

STANLEY: Gosh. I thought it was Tiffany diamonds. (*He unbuttons his shirt.*)

BLANCHE: Well, anyhow, I shall be entertained in style.

STANLEY: Uh-huh. It goes to show, you never know what is coming.

BLANCHE: Just when I thought my luck had begun to fail me . . .

STANLEY: Into the picture pops this Miami millionaire.

BLANCHE: This man is not from Miami. This man is from Dallas.

STANLEY: This man is from Dallas?

BLANCHE: Yes, this man is from Dallas where gold spouts out of the ground!

STANLEY: Well, just so he's from somewhere! (*He starts removing his shirt.*)

BLANCHE: Close the curtains before you undress any further.

STANLEY (*amiably*): This is all I'm going to undress right now. (*He rips the sack of a quart beer-bottle.*) Seen a bottle-opener?

She moves slowly towards the dresser, where she stands with her hands knotted together.

STANLEY: I used to have a cousin who could open a beer-bottle with his teeth. (*Pounding the bottle cap on the corner of table.*) That was his only accomplishment, all he could do – he was just a human bottle-opener. And then one time, at a wedding party, he broke his front teeth off! After that he was so ashamed of himself he used t' sneak out of the house when company came . . .

The bottle cap pops off and a geyser of foam shoots up.

STANLEY *laughs happily, holding up the bottle over his*

106

head.

STANLEY: Ha-ha! Rain from heaven! (*He extends the bottle towards her.*) Shall we bury the hatchet and make it a loving-cup? Huh? St wants to bury hatchet

BLANCHE: No, thank you.

STANLEY: Well, it's a red letter night for us both. You having an oil-millionaire and me having a baby.

He goes to the bureau in the bedroom and crouches to remove something from the bottom drawer.

BLANCHE (*drawing back*): What are you doing in here?

STANLEY: Here's something I always break out on special occasions like this! The silk pyjamas I wore on my wedding night! Symbolic of manhood.

BLANCHE: Oh.

STANLEY: When the telephone rings and they say, "You've got a son!" I'll tear this off and wave it like a flag! (*He shakes out a brilliant pyjama coat.*) I guess we are both entitled to put on the dog. (*He goes back to the kitchen with the coat over his arm.*)

BLANCHE: When I think of how divine it is going to be to have such a thing as privacy once more – I would weep with joy!

STANLEY: This millionaire from Dallas is not going to interfere with your privacy any? Bit more caustic

BLANCHE: It won't be the sort of thing you have in mind. This man is a gentleman and he respects me. (*Improvising feverishly.*) What he wants is my companionship. Having great wealth sometimes makes poeple lonely!

STANLEY: I wouldn't know about that. B is beginning to get to her

BLANCHE: A cultivated woman, a woman of intelligence and breeding, can enrich a man's life – immeasurably! I have those things to offer, and this doesn't take them

107

away. Physical beauty is passing. A transitory posses-
sion. But beauty of the mind and richness of the spirit
and tenderness of the heart – and I have all of those
things – aren't taken away, but grow! Increase with the
years! How strange that I should be called a destitute
woman! When I have all of these treasures locked in my
heart. (*A choked sob comes from her.*) I think of myself
as a very, very rich woman! But I have been foolish –
casting my pearls before swine!

STANLEY: Swine, huh?

BLANCHE: Yes, swine! Swine! And I'm thinking not only of
you but of your friend, Mr Mitchell. He came to see me
tonight. He dared to come here in his work-clothes! And
to repeat slander to me, vicious stories that he had
gotten from you! I gave him his walking papers . . .

STANLEY: You did, huh?

BLANCHE: But then he came back. He returned with a box
of roses to beg my forgiveness! He implored my
forgiveness. But some things are not forgivable. Deliber-
ate cruelty is not forgivable. It is the one unforgivable
thing in my opinion and it is the one thing of which I
have never, never been guilty. And so I told him, I said
to him, "Thank you," but it was foolish of me to think
that we could ever adapt ourselves to each other. Our
ways of life are too different. Our attitudes and our
backgrounds are incompatible. We have to be realistic
about such things. So farewell, my friend! And let there
be no hard feelings . . .

STANLEY: Was this before or after the telegram came from
the Texas oil millionaire?

BLANCHE: What telegram? No! No, after! As a matter of
fact, the wire came just as –

STANLEY: As a matter of fact there wasn't no wire at all!

BLANCHE: Oh, oh!

STANLEY: There isn't no millionaire! And Mitch didn't come back with roses 'cause I know where he is –

BLANCHE: Oh!

STANLEY: There isn't a goddam thing but imagination!

BLANCHE: Oh!

STANLEY: And lies and conceit and tricks!

BLANCHE: Oh!

STANLEY: And look at yourself! Take a look at yourself in that worn-out Mardi Gras outfit, rented for fifty cents from some rag-picker! And with the crazy crown on! What queen do you think you are!

BLANCHE: Oh – God . . .

STANLEY: I've been on to you from the start! Not once did you pull any wool over this boy's eyes! You come in here and sprinkle the place with powder and spray perfume and cover the light-bulb with a paper lantern, and lo and behold the place has turned into Egypt and you are the Queen of the Nile! Sitting on your throne and swilling down my liquor! I say – *Ha – Ha!* Do you hear me? *Ha – ha – ha!* (*He walks into the bedroom.*)

BLANCHE: Don't come in here!

Lurid reflections appear on the the walls around BLANCHE. *The shadows are of a grotesque and menacing form. She catches her breath, crosses to the phone and jiggles the hook.* STANLEY *goes into the bathroom and closes the door.*

BLANCHE: Operator, operator! Give me long-distance, please . . . I want to get in touch with Mr Shep Huntleigh of Dallas. He's so well-known he doesn't require any address. Just ask anybody who – Wait! – No, I couldn't find it right now . . . Please understand, I –

No! No, wait! . . . One moment! Someone is – Nothing! Hold on, please!

She sets the phone down and crosses warily into the kitchen. The night is filled with inhuman voices like cries in a jingle. The shadows and lurid reflections move sinuously as flames along the wall spaces. Through the back wall of the rooms, which have become transparent, can be seen the sidewalk. A prostitute has rolled a drunkard. He pursues her along the walk, overtakes her and there is a struggle. A policeman's whistle breaks it up. The figures disappear. Some moments later the NEGRO WOMAN *appears around the corner with a sequined bag which the prostitute had dropped on the walk. She is rooting excitedly through it.* BLANCHE *presses her knuckles to her lips and returns slowly to the phone. She speaks in a hoarse whisper.*

same thing happening inside.

BLANCHE: Operator! Operator! Never mind long-distance. Get Western Union. There isn't time to be – Western – Western Union!

She waits anxiously.

BLANCHE: Western Union? Yes! I – want to – Take down this message! "In desperate, desperate circumstances! Help me! Caught in a trap. Caught in – " *Oh!*

The bathroom door is thrown open and STANLEY *comes out in the brilliant silk pyjamas. He grins at her as he knots the tasselled sash about his waist. She gasps and backs away from the phone. He stares at her for a count of ten. Then a clicking becomes audible from the telephone, steady and rasping.*

STANLEY: You left th' phone off th' hook.

110

He crosses to it deliberately and sets it back on the hook. After he has replaced it, he stares at her again, his mouth slowly curving into a grin, and he waves between BLANCHE *and the outer door. The barely audible "blue piano" begins to drum up louder. The sound of it turns into the roar of an approaching locomotive.* BLANCHE *crouches, pressing her fists to her ears until it has gone by.*

BLANCHE (*finally straightening*): Let me – let me get by you!
STANLEY: Get by me? Sure. Go ahead. (*He moves back a pace in the doorway.*)
BLANCHE: You – you stand over there! (*She indicates a further position.*)
STANLEY (*grinning*): You got plenty of room to walk by me now.
BLANCHE: Not with you there! But I've got to get out somehow!
STANLEY: You think I'll interfere with you? Ha-ha!

The "blue piano" goes softly. She turns confusedly and makes a faint gesture. The inhuman jungle voices rise up. He takes a step towards her, biting his tongue which protrudes between his lips.

STANLEY (*softly*): Come to think of it – maybe you wouldn't be bad to – interfere with . . .

BLANCHE *moves backward through the door into the bedroom.*

BLANCHE: Stay back! Don't you come towards me another step or I'll . . .
STANLEY: What?
BLANCHE: Some awful thing will happen! It will!
STANLEY: What are you putting on now?

They are now both inside the bedroom.

BLANCHE: I warn you, don't, I'm in danger!

He takes another step. She smashes a bottle on the table and faces him, clutching the broken top.

STANLEY: What did you do that for?
BLANCHE: So I could twist the broken end in your face!
STANLEY: I bet you would do that!
BLANCHE: I would! I will if you . . .
STANLEY: Oh! So you want some rough-house! All right, let's have some rough-house!

He springs towards her, overturning the table. She cries out and strikes at him with the bottle top but he catches her wrist.

STANLEY: Tiger – tiger! Drop the bottle-top! Drop it! We've had this date with each other from the beginning!

She moans. The bottle-top falls. She sinks to her knees. He picks up her inert figure and carries her to the bed. The hot trumpet and drums from the Four Deuces sound loudly.

112

SCENE XI

It is some weeks later. STELLA *is packing* BLANCHE's *things.*
Sound of water can be heard running in the bathroom.
The portières are partly open on the poker players –
STANLEY, STEVE, MITCH *and* PABLO *– who sit around the*
table in the kitchen. The atmosphere of the kitchen is now
the same raw, lurid one of the disastrous poker night. The
building is framed by the sky of turquoise. STELLA *has*
been crying as she arranges the flowery dresses in the open
trunk. EUNICE *comes down the steps from her flat above*
and enters the kitchen. There is another burst from the
poker table.

STANLEY: Drew to an inside straight and made it, by God.

PABLO: *Maldita sea tu suerto!*

STANLEY: Put it in English, greaseball.

PABLO: I am cursing your goddam luck.

STANLEY (*prodigiously elated*): You know what luck is?
Luck is believing you're lucky. Take at Salerno. I
believed I was lucky. I figured that 4 out of 5 would not
come through but I would . . . and I did. I put that down
as a rule. To hold front position in this rat-race you've
got to believe you are lucky.

MITCH: You . . . you . . . you . . . Brag . . . brag . . . bull
. . . bull.

  STELLA *goes into the bedroom and starts folding a*
dress.

STANLEY: What's the matter with him?

EUNICE (*walking past the table*): I always did say that men
are callous things with no feelings, but this does beat
anything. Making pigs of yourselves. (*She comes through*

113

[handwritten: E is looking after baby]

the portières into the bedroom.)

STANLEY: What's the matter with her?

STELLA: How is my baby!

EUNICE: Sleeping like a little angel. Brought you some grapes. (*She puts them on a stool and lowers her voice.*) Blanche?

STELLA: Bathing.

EUNICE: How is she?

STELLA: She wouldn't eat anything but asked for a drink.

EUNICE: What did you tell her?

STELLA: I – just told her that – we'd made arrangements for her to rest in the country. She's got it mixed in her mind with Shep Huntleigh. *[handwritten: She's still living in fantasy world]*

BLANCHE *opens the bathroom door slightly.*

BLANCHE: Stella.

STELLA: Yes, Blanche?

BLANCHE: If anyone calls while I'm bathing take the number and tell them I'll call right back.

STELLA: Yes. *[handwritten: usually wears white]*

BLANCHE: That cool yellow silk – the bouclé. See if it's crushed. If it's not too crushed I'll wear it and on the lapel that silver and turquoise pin in the shape of a seahorse. You will find them in the heart-shaped box I keep my accessories in. And Stella . . . Try and locate a bunch of artificial violets in that box, too, to pin with the seahorse on the lapel of the jacket.

[handwritten: violets = purity/pure love.]

She closes the door. STELLA *turns to* EUNICE.

STELLA: I don't know if I did the right thing.

EUNICE: What else could you do?

STELLA: I couldn't believe her story and go on living with Stanley.

114 *[handwritten: very revealing. Gives us insight into what has been going on. She had to decide what was going to happen.]*

Supporting what st is saying Voice of common sense

EUNICE: Don't ever believe it. Life has got to go on. No matter what happens, you've got to keep on going.

The bathroom door opens a little.

BLANCHE (*looking out*): Is the coast clear?
STELLA: Yes, Blanche. (*To* EUNICE.) Tell her how well she's looking.
BLANCHE: Please close the curtains before I come out.
STELLA: They're closed.
STANLEY: – How many for you.
PABLO: Two. –
STEVE: – Three.

BLANCHE *appears in the amber light of the door. She has a tragic radiance in her* red satin robe *following the* sculptural lines of her body*. The "Varsouviana" rises audibly as* BLANCHE *enters the bedroom.*

under that niche.

BLANCHE (*with faintly hysterical vivacity*): I have just washed my hair.
STELLA: Did you?
BLANCHE: I'm not sure I got the soap out.
EUNICE: Such fine hair!
BLANCHE (*accepting the compliment*): It's a problem. Didn't I get a call?
STELLA: Who from, Blanche?
BLANCHE: Shep Huntleigh . . .
STELLA: Why, not yet, honey!
BLANCHE: How strange! I –

At the sound of BLANCHE*'s voice* MITCH*'s arm supporting his cards has sagged and his gaze is dissolved into space.* STANLEY *slaps him on the shoulder.* St wants to pretend

thing is going on

STANLEY: Hey, Mitch, come to!

115

[handwritten margin note: If she reacts like this to his voice after all that time it must have been worse]

The sound of this new voice shocks BLANCHE. *She makes a shocked gesture, forming his name with her lips.* STELLA *nods and looks quickly away.* BLANCHE *stands quite still for some moments – the silverbacked mirror in her hand and a look of sorrowful perplexity as though all human experience shows on her face.* BLANCHE *finally speaks with sudden hysteria.*

BLANCHE: What's going on here?

She turns from STELLA *to* EUNICE *and back to* STELLA. *Her rising voice penetrates the concentration of the game.* MITCH *ducks his head lower but* STANLEY *shoves back his chair as if about to rise.* STEVE *places a restraining hand on his arm.*

[handwritten margin note: 2 men that hurt her in some way.]

BLANCHE (*continuing*): What's happened here? I want an explanation of what's happened here.

STELLA (*agonizingly*): Hush! Hush!

EUNICE: Hush! Hush! Honey.

STELLA: Please, Blanche.

BLANCHE: Why are you looking at me like that? Is something wrong with me?

EUNICE: You look wonderful, Blanche. Don't she look wonderful?

STELLA: Yes.

EUNICE: I understand you are going on a trip.

STELLA: Yes, Blanche *is*. She's going on vacation.

EUNICE: I'm green with envy.

BLANCHE: Help me, help me get dressed!

STELLA (*handing her dress*): Is this what you –

BLANCHE: Yes, it will do! I'm anxious to get out of here – this place is a trap! *[handwritten: Ste + E are trapping her in a way]*

EUNICE: What a pretty blue jacket.

[handwritten: focus on jacket. Trying to divert her.]

STELLA: It's lilac coloured.

BLANCHE: You're both mistaken. It's Della Robbia blue. The blue of the robe in the old Madonna pictures. Are these grapes washed?

She fingers the bunch of grapes which EUNICE *has brought in.*

EUNICE: Huh?

BLANCHE: Washed, I said. Are they washed?

EUNICE: They're from the French Market.

BLANCHE: That doesn't mean they've been washed. (*The cathedral bells chime.*) Those cathedral bells – they're the only clean thing in the Quarter. Well, I'm going now. I'm ready to go.

EUNICE (*whispering*): She's going to walk out before they get here.

STELLA: Wait, Blanche.

BLANCHE: I don't want to pass in front of those men.

EUNICE: Then wait'll the game breaks up.

STELLA: Sit down and . . .

BLANCHE *turns weakly, hesitantly about. She lets them push her into a chair.*

BLANCHE: I can smell the sea air. The rest of my time I'm going to spend on the sea. And when I die, I'm going to die on the sea. You know what I shall die of? (*She plucks a grape.*) I shall die of eating an unwashed grape one day out on the ocean. I will die – with my hand in the hand of some nice-looking ship's doctor, a very young one with a small blond moustache and a big silver watch. "Poor lady," they'll say, "the quinine did her no good. That unwashed grape has transported her soul to heaven." (*The cathedral chimes are heard.*) And I'll be buried at

117

sea sewn up in a <u>clean white sack</u> and dropped overboard
– at noon – in the blaze of summer – and into an ocean as
blue as (*chimes again*) my first lover's eyes! *[handwritten: lover led to too much of this]*

[handwritten in margin: Wants it to be bright day light. No need to hide them]

A DOCTOR *and* MATRON *have appeared around the corner of
the building and climbed the steps to the porch. The
gravity of their profession is exaggerated – the unmistak-
able aura of the state institution with its cynical detach-
ment. The* DOCTOR *rings the doorbell. The murmur of the
game is interrupted.*

EUNICE (*whispering to* STELLA): That must be them.

> STELLA *presses her fist to her lips.*

BLANCHE (*rising slowly*): What is it?
EUNICE (*affectedly casual*): Excuse me while I see who's at
the door.
STELLA: Yes.

> EUNICE *goes into the kitchen.*

BLANCHE (*tensely*): I wonder if it's for me.

> *A whispered colloquy takes place at the door.*

EUNICE (*returning, brightly*): Someone is calling for Blan-
che. *[handwritten: Proves she doesn't believe what she asks]*
BLANCHE: It *is* for me, then! (*She looks fearfully from one to
the other and then to the portières. The "Varsouviana"
faintly plays.*) Is it the gentleman I was expecting from
Dallas?
EUNICE: I think it is, Blanche.
BLANCHE: I'm not quite ready.
STELLA: Ask him to wait outside.
BLANCHE: I . . .

118

EUNICE *goes back to the portières. Drums sound very softly.* tension increases

STELLA: Everything packed?
BLANCHE: My silver toilet articles are still out. reminiscent of Belle Reve
STELLA: Ah!
EUNICE (*returning*): They're waiting in front of the house.
BLANCHE: They! Who's "they"?
EUNICE: There's a lady with him.
BLANCHE: I cannot imagine who this "lady" could be! How is she dressed?
EUNICE: Just – just a sort of a – plain-tailored outfit.
BLANCHE: Possibly she's – (*Her voice dies out nervously.*)
STELLA: Shall we go, Blanche?
BLANCHE: Must we go through that room?
STELLA: I will go with you.
BLANCHE: How do I look?
STELLA: Lovely.
EUNICE (*echoing*): Lovely.

BLANCHE *moves fearfully to the portières.* EUNICE *draws them open for her.* BLANCHE *goes into the kitchen.*

BLANCHE (*to the men*): Please don't get up. I'm only passing through. reminder of what happened before

She crosses quickly to outside door. STELLA *and* EUNICE *follow. The poker players stand awkwardly at the table – all except* MITCH, *who remains seated, looking at the table.* BLANCHE *steps out on a small porch at the side of the door. She stops short and catches her breath.*

DOCTOR: How do you do?
BLANCHE: You are not the gentleman I was expecting. (*She suddenly gasps and starts back up the steps. She stops by*

119

STELLA, *who stands just outside the door, and speaks in a frightening whisper.*) That man isn't Shep Huntleigh.

The "Varsouviana" is playing distantly. STELLA *stares back at* BLANCHE. EUNICE *is holding* STELLA's *arm. There is a moment of silence – no sound but that of* STANLEY *steadily shuffling the cards.* BLANCHE *catches her breath again and slips back into the flat. She enters the flat with a peculiar smile, her eyes wide and brilliant. As soon as her sister goes past her,* STELLA *closes her eyes and clenches her hands.* EUNICE *throws her arms comfortingly about her. Then she starts up to her flat.* BLANCHE *stops just inside the door.* MITCH *keeps staring down at his hands on the table, but the other men look at her curiously. At last she starts around the table towards the bedroom. As she does,* STANLEY *suddenly pushes back his chair and rises as if to block her way. The* MATRON *follows her into the flat.*

[handwritten: E comforts Ste but not B. B's lifelines have been cut]

[handwritten: did that when he raped her]

STANLEY: Did you forget something?
BLANCHE (*shrilly*): Yes! Yes, I forgot something!

[handwritten: reminders of rape]

She rushes past him into the bedroom. Lurid reflections appear on the walls in odd, sinuous shapes. The "Varsouviana" is filtered into weird distortion, accompanied by the cries and noises of the jungle. BLANCHE *seizes the back of a chair as if to defend herself.*

STANLEY: Doc, you better go in.
DOCTOR (*motioning to the* MATRON): Nurse, bring her out.

The MATRON *advances on one side.* STANLEY *on the other. Divested of all the softer properties of womanhood, the* MATRON *is a peculiarly sinister figure in her severe dress. Her voice is bold and toneless as a fire-bell.*

[handwritten: M represents what institution is going to be like]

MATRON: Hello, Blanche.

The greeting is echoed and re-echoed by other myste- rious voices behind the walls, as if reverberated through a canyon of rock.

STANLEY: She says that she forgot something.

The echo sounds in threatening whispers.

MATRON: That's all right.
STANLEY: What did you forget, Blanche?
BLANCHE: I – I –
MATRON: It don't matter. We can pick it up later.
STANLEY: Sure. We can send it along with the trunk.
BLANCHE (*retreating in panic*): I don't know you – I don't know you. I want to be – left alone – please! *She must look mad to Matron*
MATRON: Now, Blanche!
ECHOES (*rising and falling*): Now, Blanche – now, Blanche – now, Blanche! *Now is ambiguous*
STANLEY: You left nothing here but spilt talcum and old empty perfume bottles – unless it's the paper lantern you want to take with you. You want the lantern?

He crosses to dressing-table and seizes the paper lantern, tearing it off the light bulb, and extends it towards her. She cries out as if the lantern was herself. The MATRON *steps boldly towards her. She screams and tries to break past the* MATRON. *All the men spring to their feet.* STELLA *runs out to the porch, with* EUNICE *following to comfort her, simultaneously with the confused voices of the men in the kitchen.* STELLA *rushes into* EUNICE's *embrace on the porch.*

Maybe he does not understand significance to B.

STELLA: Oh, my God, Eunice help me! Don't let them do that to her, don't let them hurt her! Oh, God, oh, please

121

God, don't hurt her! What are they doing to her? What are they doing? (*She tries to break from* EUNICE'*s arms.*)

EUNICE: No, honey, no, no, honey. Stay here. Don't go back in there. Stay with me and don't look.

STELLA: What have I done to my sister? Oh, God, what have I done to my sister? feels guilty

EUNICE: You done the right thing, the only thing you could do. She couldn't stay here; there wasn't no other place for her to go.

While STELLA *and* EUNICE *are speaking on the porch the voices of the men in the kitchen overlap them.*

STANLEY (*running in from the bedroom*): Hey! Hey! Doctor! Doctor, you better go in!

DOCTOR: Too bad, too bad. I always like to avoid it.

PABLO: This is a very bad thing.

STEVE: This is no way to do it. She should've been told.

outsiders give another dimension

PABLO: *Madre de Dios! Cosa mala, muy, muy mala!*

MITCH *has started towards the bedroom.* STANLEY *crosses to block him.* M has suddenly naked

MITCH (*wildly*): You! You done this, all o' your God damn interfering with things you –

STANLEY: Quit the blubber! (*He pushes him aside.*)

MITCH: I'll kill you! (*He lunges and strikes at* STANLEY.)

STANLEY: Hold this bone-headed cry-baby!

STEVE (*grasping* MITCH): Stop it, Mitch.

PABLO: Yeah, yeah, take it easy!

final view of Mitch
Proves to did care about B

MITCH *collapses at the table, sobbing. During the preceding scenes, the* MATRON *catches hold of* BLANCHE'*s arm and prevents her flight.* BLANCHE *turns wildly and scratches at the* MATRON. *The heavy woman pinions her*

122 out of character for M

arms. BLANCHE *cries out hoarsely and slips to her knees*.

MATRON: These fingernails have to be trimmed. (*The
DOCTOR comes into the room and she looks at him*.)
Jacket, Doctor? *Impersonal. reminds us of what will happen*
DOCTOR: Not unless necessary. *to B*

> *He takes off his hat and now becomes personalized.
> The unhuman quality goes. His voice is gentle and
> reassuring as he crosses to BLANCHE and crouches in front
> of her. As he speaks her name, her terror subsides a little.
> The lurid reflections from the walls, the inhuman cries* She is
> *and noises die out and her own hoarse crying is calmed.* calming down

DOCTOR: Miss DuBois. *B has always wanted respect from men*

> *She turns her face to him and stares at him with
> desperate pleading. He smiles; then he speaks to the
> MATRON.*

DOCTOR: It won't be necessary.
BLANCHE (*faintly*): Ask her to let go of me.
DOCTOR (*to the MATRON*): Let go.

> *The MATRON releases her. BLANCHE extends her hands
> towards the DOCTOR. He draws her up gently and
> supports her with his arm and leads her through the
> portières.*

BLANCHE (*holding tight to his arm*): Whoever you are – I
have always depended on the kindness of strangers.
In contrast to family. Reminds of strangemen in hotel.

> *The poker players stand back as BLANCHE and the
> DOCTOR cross the kitchen to the front door. She allows
> him to lead her as if she were blind. As they go out on the
> porch, STELLA cries out her sister's name from where she
> is crouched a few steps upon the stairs.*

STELLA: Blanche! Blanche! Blanche!

[handwritten: As though ste has lost her forever]

BLANCHE *walks on without turning, followed by the* DOCTOR *and the* MATRON. *They go around the corner of the building.* EUNICE *descends to* STELLA *and places the child in her arms. It is wrapped in a pale blue blanket.* STELLA *accepts the child, sobbingly.* EUNICE *continues downstairs and enters the kitchen where the men except for* STANLEY, *are returning silently to their places about the table.* STANLEY *has gone out on the porch and stands at the foot of the steps looking at* STELLA.

[handwritten: shows ste what she has to look forward to]

[handwritten: Baby a symbol of the future]

STANLEY (*a bit uncertainly*): Stella? [handwritten: Not sure anymore]

She sobs with inhuman abandon. There is something luxurious in her complete surrender to crying now that her sister is gone. [handwritten: had to be strong for B]

STANLEY (*voluptuously, soothingly*): Now, honey. Now, love. Now, now love. (*He knells beside her and his fingers find the opening of her blouse.*) Now, now, love. Now, love . . .

The luxurious sobbing, the sensual murmur fade away under the swelling music of the "blue piano" and the muted trumpet. [handwritten: How does stella react?]

STEVE: This game is seven-card stud.

[handwritten: The game is over?   Stanley .]

CURTAIN

[handwritten: What kind of future is there for stella + Stanley? Can it be like it used to be?]

124

ACTIVITIES AND EXPLORATIONS

A Keeping Track

A series of questions, scene by scene, intended to stimulate the beginnings of a response to the play. Used during the course of a first reading of the play, for writing or discussion, the questions will help you to keep track of character development, plot, themes and the writer's techniques. They should also be useful as a preparation for the more detailed coursework assignments suggested in **Explorations**. You could use the questions as a basis for a 'journal' of your responses to the play.

Scene I

1 Look closely at the first long stage direction. How does Tennessee Williams use the sights, sounds and suggestions of smells to create a particular atmosphere? What atmosphere do you think he is trying to create?

2 The first visual impressions of Stanley, Stella and Blanche are important. What impression do you get of Stella and Stanley from their first brief appearance? Why is Blanche described as "incongruous"?

3 In a stage direction, the writer describes Blanche's manner as suggesting "a moth". What do you *associate* with a moth?

4 The place names used in the play have obviously been chosen carefully. Discuss, or note down, your associations with, or reactions to: Desire, Cemeteries, Elysian Fields and Belle Reve.

5 Why is Blanche visiting her sister?

6 What do you learn of Blanche's past?

7 How is Blanche recieved by Stanley? Do you feel a tension between them? If so, why do you think that tension is there?

8 Look at the last few lines of the scene. The sound of a cat screeching and polka music are used. Why?

9 What makes Blanche feel ill at the end of the scene?

Scene II

1 Is there anything in this scene which suggests the childhood relationship between Blanche and Stella? Are either of them trying to recreate that relationship in the present?

2 Why does Stella try to advise (tell) Stanley how to behave towards Blanche?

3 What does Stanley suspect Blanche of? How do you react to his references to the law, and to "acquaintances" who can "appraise" Blanche's possessions?

4 Describe the contents of Blanche's trunk.

5 Who do you think 'wins' the encounter between Blanche and Stanley? Give reasons for your answer.

6 Why do you think Stanley tells Blanche about the expected baby – when Stella had earlier asked him not to?

7 During this scene we learn more about Belle Reve. What are we told?

Scene III

1 Tennessee Williams called an earlier version of this play, *The Poker Night*. Discuss, or note down, what you associate with the game of poker.

2   Why is Stanley on his "high horse" at the beginning of the scene? *because he's winning*

3   How are Blanche and Stella received when they return? *in a sexist way*

4   Why do you think Stanley is annoyed when Mitch leaves the game?

5   Blanche says she thinks she might "bathe". You will notice that she bathes a good deal during the play. Why, do you think?

6   What impression does Blanche try to give Mitch about herself?

7   What do you learn of Mitch's background? Why do you think he is attracted to Blanche? Why is she attracted to him? *he is different to all the rest*

8   What is Stanley's reaction to the radio? Why do you think he reacts so strongly?

9   Does the contrast between the atmosphere in the bedroom and the atmosphere in the main room of the apartment strike you as particularly interesting? What are the differences?

10 How do the various characters react to Stanley's violence?

11 Describe how Stanley gets Stella to come back from the Hubbels' apartment.

12 Why does she return?

Scene IV

1   Stella tries to explain to Blanche the nature of her relationship with Stanley. Of his violence she says, "I was – sort of – thrilled by it." What do you think she means?

2   Can you identify in Stella's explanation any statements

127

which seem to you to sum up how her relationship with Stanley works?

3 What is Blanche's plan for Stella's future?

4 Blanche contrasts the world of Belle Reve with Stella's present life style. Can you identify the main differences between the two worlds?

5 Stanley listens in on some of this conversation. Why do you think there is the sound of a locomotive in the distance as he first appears on the stage? Why do you think he does not immediately go into the room with Blanche and Stella?

6 Is Stella tempted to leave Stanley at any point during this scene?

7 When Stanley eventually does enter the room he embraces Stella and smiles at Blanche. What does that smile mean?

8 The scene ends with the sound of the "blue piano" – which is used regularly in the play. What do you think this particular music signifies?

Scene V

1 It is possible to see Steve and Eunice Hubbel as an extreme version of Stella and Stanley, (or some sort of indication of what Stanley and Stella might become). Do you think this view is justified? Is the fact that they own the building in which the two couples live of any significance? Contrast Eunice and Steve's way of life with the sort of life which Blanche and Stella lived in their past.

2 Do you think the star signs of Stanley and Blanche are appropriate? Why?

3 Why does Tenessee Williams have the sound of thunder

heard in the distance at one point during this scene?

4 The stage directions in this scene emphasise Blanche's "fear" and "panic". What is she afraid of?

5 What does Blanche reveal about herself in the speech beginning, "I was never hard or self-sufficient enough"?

6 What does Blanche tell us, during this scene, about why she needs Mitch and how she will 'catch' him?

7 Why does Blanche behave as she does towards the young man who appears at the door? Does what happens in any way connect with what she was saying earlier? Does she see in this young man something that she has lost?

Scene VI

1 We are given the impression at the beginning of this scene that the evening has not worked all that well for Blanche or Mitch. Look closely at their conversation during the first part of the scene. Does the nature of that conversation help explain why their evening has not been a great success so far?

2 What do you learn about Mitch's mother and how he feels about her?

3 Blanche's story about Allan and Moon Lake Casino is possibly at the centre of this scene – and maybe at the centre of the whole play, (Scene VI is about halfway through the play). Why are these events important to Blanche? How have they shaped her life since?

4 Is this story part of Blanche's strategy to "catch" Mitch – or is it closer to her "real" self?

5 What do Mitch and Blanche have in common?

6 Look at the last line of the scene – "Sometimes – there's God – so quickly." Blanche is seeing (or feeling) a

religious meaning in something. What do you think had induced this response?

Scene VII

1 How would you describe Blanche's mood at the beginning of this scene? How would you explain this mood?
2 What does Stanley reveal about Blanche's past?
3 Stanley's revelations are punctuated by the sound of Blanche singing in the bathroom. Why does Tennessee Williams organise the scene in this way?
4 What do you think Stanley's motives are in telling Stella about Blanche's recent past?
5 How does Stella react to what she learns?
6 What do you think Tennessee Williams wants you to feel about Stanley during this scene? What does he want you to feel for Blanche?

Scene VIII

1 Does Mitch's absence contribute significantly to this scene? Why has he not turned up? What does his absence tell you about Stanley? Could you justify what Stanley has done? What do you learn about Mitch from his absence?
2 How does Blanche try to cope with Stanley? Does she succeed – as she did in Scene II?
3 Why does Stanley bristle when Blanche uses the word, 'Polack'?
4 How cruel do you think Stanley is being? (Do you think he feels at all guilty about his behaviour – or proud of himself? Find evidence to justify your answer.)

5 What do you think the coming baby means to Stanley?
6 What part do the telephone calls play in the structure of the scene? (Why has Tennessee Williams put them into the scene?)

Scene IX

1 Why has Mitch come to see Blanche?
2 Why is the polka tune so insistent during the first part of the scene?
3 Blanche says, at one point, "I don't want realism." Describe how she tries to maintain her illusions during the scene.
4 What does Blanche say she wanted from Mitch?
5 What do you think is the importance of the flower vendor's calls from the street? What is dead?
6 How have they 'failed' each other?

Scene X

1 Why does Blanche break the mirror?
2 Why do you think Stanley undermines the reality of the Shep Huntleigh story and of Mitch's supposed apology?
3 Stanley talks of waving his pyjama top like a flag when he hears of the birth of the baby. Is his choice of "flag" significant?
4 What are his motives in raping Blanche? (Does the rape indicate sexual attraction or something more – something different? Why does he say "We've had this date with each other from the beginning"?
5 The rape is accompanied by the music of the "blue piano". Why?

Scene XI

1 Do you think Stella knows about the rape? Is there any evidence in this scene to suggest an answer to this question?

2 How do you explain Blanche's retreat into madness?

3 What comment do you think Tennessee Williams is making in his organisation of the characters in the scene – the women with Blanche – the men playing cards?

4 How does Blanche's long speech about death draw together the main elements of her illusions?

5 How does the doctor manage to calm Blanche and lead her out?

6 How do you react to Blanche's last words before she leaves?

7 What do the last few moments of the play (after Blanche has gone) suggest to you about Stanley and Stella's future?

B Explorations

1 Stories

a) Tell the story of Blanche and Allan – how they met, ran away and what happened when they returned. Use Blanche's description at the end of Scene VI to help you, but add as much detail from your imagination as you can.

b) Tell they story of Mitch and Blanche from Mitch's point of view. Include at least one scene in which Mitch talks to his mother about Blanche.

2 Scenes

a) Write a scene in which Stella and Eunice discuss the events of Scene X in the play (the rape). How does Stella react to Blanche's allegations? How does she come to decide that Blanche must be committed to an institution? How does Eunice help her shape her decisions?

b) Write a scene between Blanche and the doctor, some weeks after leaving her sister's apartment. How does she explain the events? Is she truthful – or does she convert the events into an illusion?

3 Reports

a) Write a report from the high school superintendent (Mr Graves) to his school governors in which he assesses Blanche's character, her ability as a teacher and gives his reasons for dismissing her.

b) Write the doctor's report on Blanche. What does he know about her past? How does he assess her condition? What does he think her long term future is?

(*Note:* Tennessee Williams says Blanche has a 'neurasthenic personality' – see notes and glossary at the end of the play.)

4   Letters

a) Write a letter from Stella to Blanche – some years after the end of the play. Is Blanche still in an institution? How is Stella's marriage? Have the events of the play had a long term effect on Stella and Stanley?

b) Write a letter from Blanche to Shep Huntleigh shortly after the events of the play. How does she describe the recent past and her present position? Is she asking him to 'rescue' her from the institution?

5   Design brief

Put together a 'design brief' for a production of the play. Outline your ideas on set design (with sketches), your advice on costume (with character notes) and your thoughts on use of sound. Justify your choices with evidence from the actual script.

Character Studies

Blanche

Her past

a) What do you learn of Blanche's early life from Stella's defence of her in Scene VII?

b) How did Blanche lose Belle Reve? What does Blanche say about the deaths in the family, (in

Scene I)? How important are these two experiences to her?

c) The story of Blanche's relationship with Allan gradually unfolds during the course of the play – in Scene I, Scene II, Scene VI and Scene IX. Outline the main events of their relationship and describe how these have shaped Blanche's life since Allan's death.

d) How are Blanche's past actions, particularly in Laurel after the death of Allan, in conflict with the way she would like to be seen?

e) Consider the following comment:

'*A Streetcar Named Desire* makes it clear that for Williams the act of fleeing always becomes the act of reliving the past. Flight forces the presence of the past on his characters as the presence of what they attempted to flee.'

(Donald Pease in *Tennessee Williams: A Tribute*)

Do the 'onstage' events of the play seem to you to be repeating any of the events in Blanche's past life? being let down by people

Her illusions

a) What is Blanche's attitude towards alcohol? (Why does she drink? Why does she try to conceal her drinking?)

b) Why do Blanche's clothes and jewellery mean so much to her? cares about what people think.

c) Why does she bathe so often? feels dirty

d) At one point in the play Blanche says, "I don't tell the truth. I tell what ought to be the truth," (Scene IX). What does Blanche think, "ought to be the truth"?

135

fantasy security

e) What does Shep Huntleigh mean to Blanche?

f) Look at Blanche's long speech about death in Scene XI. Identify the main elements in the speech and show how they summarise Blanche's vision of what "ought to be the truth".

Her loneliness and isolation

a) Does the way Blanche speaks in any way isolate her from those around her?

b) Do her values (what she thinks is important in life) alienate her from the people she meets?

need for security

c) What draws Blanche and Mitch together?

d) What does she want from Mitch? Do you think the kind of relationship she hopes for is possible?

e) Can you justify the view that Blanche's last words in the play ("I have always depended on the kindness of strangers") are a perfect expression of the sort of life she has led?

Her contradictions

a) What does she think of the physical relationship between Stanley and Stella? *jealous of it*

b) How does she use her own sexuality – and to what purpose? (Look at her conversation with Stanley in Scene II and the speech beginning, "I never was hard or self sufficient enough. . . ", in Scene V)

c) Do your answers to (a) and (b) above reveal a contradiction in Blanche's approach to men?

d) Now that you have read the whole play, how fitting do you think that early description of her being like a "moth" is?

e) Do you think Stanley's rape of Blanche causes her final withdrawal into madness?

Afraid of light.

Stanley

a) In an early stage direction Tennessee Williams describes Stanley as, "the gaudy seed-bearer". What do you think he means by this?

b) Similarly, Stanley's star sign is Capricorn. What does this imply?

c) Why do you think Stanley's actions are often accompanied by a blue piano/trumpet and drums, or the sound of a locomotive? *sexy, unpredictable*

d) Describe Stanley's love for Stella. Does he patronise her? Is he tender? Is it a selfish love? Does he need her? When are they at their happiest? Does she have to suppress any of her natural qualities? *?*

e) Do you think he feels threatened by Blanche's arrival? If so, how? *yes, for Stella's affections.*

f) How important is the idea of 'being master in his own house' to Stanley? *very. He is proud*

g) What do you think of his talk of the law and of worldly wise acquaintances? *not educated so mixes with educated people*

h) Why does he go out of his way to be uncouth to Blanche?

i) How does he 'use' the expected baby? *to regain his pride*

j) Can you see any similarity in the way he treats Stella and the way he treats Mitch? *patronizes?*

k) How does his use of the English language contrast sharply with the way Blanche speaks?

l) Why is he sensitive about being called a "Polack"? *v. nationalist. cowardice towards ...*

m) Why does he challenge Blanche's illusions? Why does he rape her? *to show who's in charge. re: baby*

n) Do you think he feels any guilt after raping Blanche? *yes*

o) Do your sympathies for Stanley alter during the course of the play? *yes*

137

p) A recent critic said "Stanley is Williams's vision of the rapacity of the life force and the pragmatism of survival." Can you supply evidence to justify this statement?

Stella

a) Find evidence to support the view that Blanche tries to make Stella a child again. *see beginning*

b) How does Blanche try to undermine Stella's marriage? Does Stella ever go along with what Blanche says?

c) In Scene IV Stella explains the nature of her relationship with Stanley. What does she say? *sex*

d) What *price* does Stella have to pay for her continuing marriage to Stanley? *sister*

e) Does Stella change during the course of the play?

Mitch

a) What does Mitch represent to Blanche?

b) Mitch is part of Stanley's world. What does he share with Stanley? How is he treated by Stanley? In what ways is he different?

c) How important is Mitch's mother to him?

d) What draws Mitch and Blanche together?

e) How difficult does he find the early 'courtship' of Blanche?

f) Why does he reject Blanche? What does this say about his character?

g) What do you think of his behaviour towards Blanche in Scene IX?

h) How do you think he will feel in the future about Blanche? *pity*

   i) How important is the inscription in Mitch's cigarette case? What does it tell you about the nature of his relationships?

An introduction to themes

Presented here are a series of quotations, together with brief notes, which might be used as a starting point for exploring some of the themes which concern Tennessee Williams in *A Streetcar Named Desire*.

   A useful approach could be to consider the quotations and notes, illustrate or support them with evidence from the play, and attempt some evaluation of the relative importance of the suggested themes in the play. Specific essay questions are included in the last section of **Coursework Assignments.**

   The themes proposed are by no means exhaustive, and it may well be that you will discover and explore what to you will appear more obvious, more important or more interesting approaches to what you perceive to be Tennessee Williams's central concerns.

1 The past

"Everyone carries around all the selves that they have ever been, intact, waiting to be reactivated in moments of pain, of fear, of danger. Everything is retrievable, every shock, every hurt. But perhaps it becomes a duty to abandon the stock of time that one carries within oneself, to discard it in favour of the present, so that one's embrace may be turned outwards to the world in which one has made one's home."

(From *Latecomers,* the novel by Anita Brookner, 1988)

"*A Streetcar Named Desire* makes it clear that for Williams the act of fleeing always becomes the act of reliving the past. Flight forces the presence of the past on his characters as the presence of what they attempt to flee."

(Donald Pease in *Tennessee Williams: A Tribute*)

Note: see the questions on Blanche's past in **Coursework assignments: Character Studies.**

2 Death

"Death is my best theme, don't you think? The pain of dying is what worries me, not the act. After all, nobody gets out of life alive."

(Tennessee Williams to a reporter in 1963).

Notes: Look again at what Blanche has to say about dying in Scenes I and XI.

love +
security

Consider what Blanche loses when she loses Belle Reve and Allan. How important is the intervention of the flower vendor in Scene IX?

How much do you read into the inscription in Mitch's cigarette case?

Is there a connection between dying and madness?

streetcars

3 The South

(i) "I write out of love for the South . . . It is out of a regret for a South that no longer exists that I write of the forces that have destoyed it."

(Tennessee Williams, quoted by his mother in *Remember Me To Tom.*)

(ii) ". . . you knew you were passing through a ruined kingdom. The myths, even in the moment you discovered them, were worm eaten . . . The lawns

and columned porticos were never far from the
tangled swamps with odd flowers . . . And always
drifting against the sky were the long grey-white
tufts of Spanish moss on spreading live-oak trees.
The live-oak was indeed a creepy symbol of the
South, for in the sunlight and at a distance it was a
majestic sight, and the Spanish moss trailed from
its branches like the plumes of a jousting knight.
As you get closer, the knight was slightly fly-blown.
In the twilight the moss was a grey fuzz . . . and
you saw that it was a parasite clinging to the outline
of a healthy tree."

(Alistair Cooke in *Talk About America*, 1968)

(iii) "The Southern accent gives *Streetcar* its music, its
irony, its lyrical plangency, its curiously decadent
tone. These are not to be found on the page, silent.
They are in that pervasive, strong, clinging accent
which has so much of dispossession in it. Williams's
play are full of dispossessed people who we feel
were once gentle but who find the jungle has
caught up with their gracious clearings and spaces
and the animals with their civilized pursuits. We
hear in it, too, a kind of self-defeat, self-delusion, a
weakness, so that we wonder what lies behind the
gentleness, the civil behaviour."

(Gareth Lloyd Evans in *The Language of Modern
Drama*, 1977)

Note: Some critics have noted that the battle between
Blanche and Stanley is the conflict between the old
world values of the South (see Blanche in Scene X, the
speech beginning, "A cultivated woman . . . ") and the
aggressive materialism of the newer urban world.

4 Survival

(i) "The play, and its author, beg the question of the price of survival."

(ii) "His idea of heaven had turned into a hell of his own making."

(John Lahr, from an artical on Tennessee Williams in *The Guardian*, 2.2.88.)

Note: Look at each of the characters and consider what they see as their salvation. Who 'survives' the events of the play? Who fails to survive? What is the price of their survival?

Critical essay titles

1 How concerned are each of the four characters with their own survival? Discuss their needs and how they go about fulfilling them, and evaluate their success in terms of surviving the events of the play.

2 Write a guide for two actors about to play Stanley and Blanche. Advise the actors on what you see as the two characters' main concerns. How do they behave towards each other and towards Stella and Mitch? Why do they behave in this way? Do they change as the play progresses? (It might help you to focus your ideas if you were to select two scenes and analyse them in detail.)

3 Discuss the importance of symbolism in *A Streetcar Named Desire*.

4 How are the past and the present intertwined in *A Streetcar Named Desire*.

5 "Williams has a very strong aural sense . . . a putting together of 'heard' and 'seen' materials." Illustrate this point (made by Gareth Lloyd Evans in *The Language of Modern Drama*) paying particular attention to Wil-

liams's use of set design, sound effects and the language used by the main characters.

6 Discuss the view that *A Streetcar Named Desire* is a play concerned with the conflict between the values of the old world and the new, and that this conflict is expressed through the battle between Stanley and Blanche.

7 Which character (or characters) do you think Tennessee Williams felt closest to in his play? Do what you perceive to be his feelings coincide with your own?

8 What do you believe Tennessee Williams is saying about human sexuality in *A Streetcar Named Desire*?

Glossary and notes

Epigram   This is from a poem by Hart Crane (1829–1932), an American poet who committed suicide in 1932. It provides a complex and interesting introduction to the major themes of the play.

Scene I

Elysian Fields	in Greek mythology this was the place heroes went to after death.
L & N tracks:	a railway line for the Louisiana and Nashville Railroad.
white frame:	buildings of wood in the French colonial style.
'blue piano':	black American blues music, used by Williams as a symbol for Stanley's primitive life force.
'Red hots!':	Frankfurter sausages heavily spiced.
a Blue Moon cocktail:	a whiskey based cocktail.
a poor boy's sandwhich:	bread, mutton and pickles.
a valise:	a small suitcase.
Desire/Cemeteries:	place names in New Orleans – which really exist. A streetcar is a tramcar.
Por nada:	no trouble.
Belle Reve:	beautiful dream.
Poe:	Edgar Allan Poe (1809–49) writer of supernatural stories and poetry.
woodland of Weir:	From Poe's poem, *Ulalume*.
high school superintendent:	the senior school administrator.
wire:	telegram.
a feather bob:	a particular hairstyle – the hair cut in layers giving it a feathery lightness.
Polacks:	slang for Polish.

Jax:	Jacksonville.
screen door:	an outer door with mosquito-wire see-through panels.
gaudy seed-bearer:	male, 'macho', showy, crude.
Laurel:	Blanche's home town in Mississippi.
not in my territory:	a) not in the area where Stanley is a salesman; b) outside the world he recognises.

Scene II		
	toilette:	make-up *etc.*
	monkey doings:	behaving in a silly way.
	Galatoires:	a French restaurant in the French quarter of New Orleans.
	Napoleonic Code:	after Napoleon III of France; the husband had ownership of the wife's possessions. Louisiana was formerly a French colony.
	Lemon-coke:	coca-cola and lemonade.
	re-bop:	trivial and evasive chatter.
	epic fornications:	large scale immorality.
	tamale vendor:	a person who sells hot and spicy Mexican food.
	hot trumpet:	evocative jazz played on a trumpet.

Scene III		
	portieres:	an internal doorway covering, *eg* curtains.
	one-eyed jacks:	the jack of spades and the jack of hearts – seen in profile on a playing card, showing only one eye.
	ante up:	raise the stakes.
	a sugar-tit:	a baby's teat coated in sugar.

	kibitz:	to watch and advise a card player.
	Xavier Cugat:	a popular band leader of the time, (late nineteen forties America).
	the "head":	lavatory.
	quarters:	twenty five cent coins.
	wrapper:	dressing gown.
	Mrs Browning:	English poet, Elizabeth Barrett Browning (1806–61).
	Bourbon:	a street in New Orleans know for jazz and striptease clubs.
	bobby-soxers:	adolescent girls.
	Hawthorne:	American writer, Nathaniel Hawthorne, (1804–64).
	Whitman:	American poet, Walt Whitman (1819–82).
	Wien, Wien, nur du allein:	a Viennese waltz.
	Potomac:	a river.
Scene IV	**wore his pin:**	a young man in the United States would give a 'pin' to a girl as a token of his commitment to the relationship.
	bromo:	bromide – to calm nerves.
Scene V	**turn the trick:**	attract men.
	fading:	her looks are going; she is aging.
	put out:	be obviously enticing.
	dime:	a ten cent coin.
	fifteen of seven:	a quarter to seven.
	Rosenkavalier:	the hero of a popular opera by Richard Strauss.
Scene VI	**neurasthenic personality:**	suffering from a nervous disability.
	Lake Pontchartrain:	an amusement park near New Orleans.

Mae West:	a film star known for her 'large' figure, her use of witty sexual innuendo.
owl car:	an all night tramcar.
Pleiades:	the star constellation 'Seven Sisters'.
Bohemian:	unconventional lifestyle.
"Je suis la Dame aux Camellias! Vous etes – Armand!"	I am the Lady of Camellias. You are Armand. A well known romance in which a courtesan is 'saved' by love but later dies of TB.
"Voulez-vous couchez avec moi ce soir? Vous ne comprenez pas? Ah, quel dommage!":	Would you like to go to bed with me this evening? Don't you understand? What a pity!
wash-coat:	a jacket of light material.
Loew's State:	a cinema.
Two-forty-first:	an army unit.

Scene VII	**100 on the nose:**	exactly 100 degrees Fahrenheit.
	no lily:	not an innocent.
	Barnum and Bailey:	a circus.
	ordinance:	something like a court order.
	Possess your soul in patience:	A quotation from *Hamlet*.

Scene VIII	**empty lot:**	Waste ground.
	my beau:	admirer/boyfriend.
	cursed a blue streak:	swear a lot.
	Huey Long:	Governor of Louisiana, assasinated in 1928, and remembered for his abuse of power.
	get the coloured lights going:	sexual passion.
	Varsouviana:	the polka tune which Blanche associates with Allan's death.

	"El pan de mais" etc:	A Mexican folk song; the words mean 'maize bread with no salt'.
Scene IX	**robe:**	dressing gown.
	boxed out of your mind:	very drunk.
	"Flores para los muertos":	flowers for the dead.
	"Corones para les muertos":	coronets for the dead.
Scene X	**the glass cracks:**	seen as an omen of misfortune.
	ATO:	Auxiliary Territorial Officer.
	Tiffany:	expensive jewellers in New York.
	put on the dog:	dress up for a special occasion.
	Mardi Gras outfit:	a carnival costume.
Scene XI	**Maldita sea tu suerto:**	curses on your luck.
	Salerno:	Second World War battle (in Italy).
	Madre de Dios etc:	Mother of God. This is a bad, bad, business.

THE HEREFORD PLAYS
General Editor: E. R. Wood

John Arden
Serjeant Musgrave's Dance

Alan Ayckbourn
Confusions

Peter Barnes
The Ruling Class

Robert Bolt
A Man for All Seasons

Bertolt Brecht
The Caucasian Chalk Circle

Chapman and Coxe
Billy Budd

Brian Clark
Whose Life Is It Anyway?

Shelagh Delaney
A Taste of Honey

Nikolai Gogol
The Government Inspector

Greenwood and Gow
Love on the Dole

Willis Hall
The Long and the Short and the Tall

Stanley Houghton
Hindle Wakes

Henrik Ibsen
An Enemy of the People

D. H. Lawrence
The Widowing of Mrs Holroyd and The Daughter-in-Law

Arthur Miller
The Crucible
Death of a Salesman
All My Sons
A View From the Bridge

Bill Naughton
Spring and Port Wine

André Obey
Noah

John Patrick
The Teahouse of the August Moon

Luigi Pirandello
Six Characters in Search of an Author

Stephen Poliakoff
City Sugar

J. B. Priestley
An Inspector Calls
When We Are Married

R. C. Sherriff
Journey's End

David Storey
In Celebration

J. M. Synge
The Playboy of the Western World and *Riders to the Sea*

John Whiting
A Penny for a Song

Oscar Wilde
The Importance of Being Earnest

Emlyn Williams
The Corn is Green
Night Must Fall

Tennessee Williams
The Glass Menagerie
A Streetcar Named Desire

THEMES

DEATH

① Mexican seller of tin flowers for decorating coffins + graves is the symbolic figure of death. eg. of the expressionist element of the play, an attempt by Williams to convey outwardly what is occurring in minds of the characters.

② Death of Belle Reve lst.

③ Death of Alan plays crucial part in Blanche's life. His tragic death is at first only dimly perceived by the audience but gradually, as truth becomes known, we see his death as the obvious, acceptable explanation of Blanche's instability.

MADNESS

① Blanche is fearful of going mad from the beginning. She shows a constant awareness of slipping of controls, of a temptation to let go. All the classic symptoms are there - fits of embarrassingly forced gaiety, sudden panic, withdrawal into unreality and need for alcohol as a way of not remembering.

② Clearly, she herself is aware of her fragile mental state. She retreats into fantasy world when Stanley becomes increasingly abusive. This can be seen as initial stage in her madness in which she creates her own reality in order to remove herself from a world with which she cannot cope.

FATE + PASSION.

① Title - streetcar moving along the rails to its destination and unable to change its course is a fitting symbol of a relentless inevitability of a fate which cannot be avoided. Desire, or sexual passion, is the moving force that carries the heroine to her fate.

② Helplessness of the individual against the fate that is foreordained by his or her nature and weaknesses of character is also symbolised by image of moth, so fatally attracted to flame of passion.